MENU
For Life

An easy-to-use
cookbook and meal plan
for healthy eating
and entertaining

**Joan Klun Kaye
and L.E. Smith, M.A., R.D.**

*Illustrated by Denise L. McGee
Photographs by Rick Smith*

HEALTH FOCUS, INC.
ROCHESTER, MICHIGAN

HEALTH FOCUS, INC.
P.O. Box 8113
Rochester, Michigan 48308

Library of Congress Catalog Card Number
87-91256

Produced by Wolcott and Redstone, Inc.
Birmingham, Michigan

Printed by Thomson-Shore, Inc.
Dexter, Michigan

ISBN 0-9619172-0-2

The information in this book is true and complete to the
best knowledge of the authors. This book is in no way
intended to replace or conflict with the advice given by
a personal physician. The authors and publisher disclaim
all liability in connection with the use of this book.

To all who seek to improve
the health and quality of their lives.

CONTENTS

Foreword   vii
Preface   ix
Acknowledgements   xi
How to Use This Book   1
Soups and Sauces   5
Salads and Dressings   27
Vegetables   47
Meatless Meals   57
Poultry, Fish and Meat   73
Grains and Fillings   97
Desserts and Beverages   113
Four-Week Menu Plan   127
Index   145
Abbreviations   (inside front cover)
Dietary Guidelines   (inside back cover)

This book is an excellent reflection, in recipe form, of the philosophy of the Meadow Brook Health Enhancement Institute of Oakland University, Rochester, Michigan.

Among the institute's primary goals are teaching program participants how to reduce the risk of chronic, degenerative diseases, such as diabetes, coronary artery disease, hypertension and obesity, and how to enhance their feelings of well-being.

A balanced diet low in fat content is an important component of a lifestyle designed to improve and maintain good health. Current research indicates that nutrition plays an extremely important role in controlling, treating and preventing many degenerative diseases.

This volume offers an excellent starting point for individuals concerned about lowering their fat consumption, balancing their diet, losing weight, reducing their risk of certain health problems, and improving their overall health. It includes recipes for lowering total fat, particularly saturated fat, increasing complex carbohydrates, and moderating the daily consumption of protein and sodium.

For years, we have been advising our program participants to modify their diets, based on our own rigorous dietary guidelines. However, we had difficulty referring them to one source for the specifics of *how* to change their eating habits because few of the cookbooks we were aware of treated the subject in a thorough manner. *Menu for Life* fills this information void and does it in practical, readable language. I feel confident that it will be an excellent source for our program participants.

I recommend this cookbook to all who are seeking to improve their eating habits, thereby reducing the risk of preventable, disabling diseases, and potentially improving the quality of their lives.

FRED W. STRANSKY, Ph.D.
Director
Meadow Brook Health Enhancement Institute
Oakland University
Rochester, Michigan

enu for Life is the happy outcome of a meeting between two people with different but complementary interests in preparing good food.

As a registered dietitian and a clinical nutritionist at the Meadow Brook Health Enhancement Institute of Oakland University, Rochester, Michigan, my primary aim has been to apply my background in nutrition and food science toward counseling and educating individuals seeking to improve their eating habits. Joan Klun Kaye is a homemaker with a creative genius for combining ingredients that result in tasty, attractive and healthy meals. Our meeting at the institute began the process of combining my expertise in the science of foods with Joan's considerable culinary skill.

We met shortly after Joan became a participant in the institute's Health Maintenance/Health Improvement program. As her interest and knowledge in health promotion grew, she quickly began to question the traditional methods of food preparation in which she was well-versed. She discovered something I had long known: cookbooks that combined sound, complete nutritional information with meals that tasted good and were easy to prepare were practically nonexistent. Soon, Joan was devising her own recipes. She asked me if they were nutritionally sound—and, if not, how they should be altered. I began computing nutritional analyses of her recipes for closer evaluation; she took my recommendations back to her kitchen for revisions.

We quickly realized we were on to something, and that something would become *Menu for Life*.

Joan and I began to plan a cookbook that would feature all the elements we felt were missing in other books. Foremost, we included serving sizes with specific nutritional data (on such vital areas as protein, calcium, iron, sodium, dietary fiber, calories and percentages of fat and carbohydrates) for each recipe. In keeping with the U.S. Department of Agriculture and U.S. Department of Health and Human Services' Dietary Guidelines for Americans, we strove to reduce the percentage of fat in each recipe (most are less than 20%), to lower the amount of total fat, to reduce the sources of saturated fat, to moderate protein levels, and to increase the amount of complex carbohydrates.

As busy women, we were determined to streamline every recipe, and to devise meals that fit today's on-the-move style of eating. We also knew that many people mistakenly believe healthy food can't taste or look good enough to serve to guests, and they leave behind their good intentions when pressed for time or the need to entertain. We wanted to develop recipes that would remove those stumbling blocks.

Joan insisted that each recipe be appealing to both the eye and appetite. I was equally committed to ensuring each meet our firm dietary guidelines. Our balancing act resulted in 111 recipes we are proud to live with. We hope *Menu for Life* provides the foundation for a lifelong diet you can live with, too.

L.E. SMITH, M.A., R.D.

ACKNOWLEDGEMENTS

I am deeply grateful to my dear family and
friends, including L.E. Smith, who sampled my food,
gave their honest but encouraging comments, and
supported me fully in this work.

JOAN KLUN KAYE

MENU
For Life
COOKBOOK

The recipes in this book look different from those in most —and there's good reason for it. They provide far more information than you will find in other cookbooks—the kind of information that gives new perspective to meal preparation.

At hand is not only a list of ingredients and directions for preparation, but information that can help you plan all the meals for your day, determine appropriate accompaniments, calculate the time needed to prepare each dish, and analyze the nutrient quality of your chosen recipe. This is the kind of information nutrition-conscious people have been waiting for!

Following are tips on how to interpret the information given in each recipe.

HOW TO USE YOUR COOKBOOK

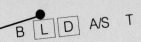

B L D A/S T

Meals: These symbols indicate that the recipe is suggested for breakfast (B), lunch (L), dinner (D) or as an appetizer or snack (A/S). Recipes that travel well (T) pack easily in lunches or coolers, or can be taken from the freezer at home to a microwave oven at work.

HEALTHY BURRITOS

*1 c. cooked kidney beans
  2 tsp. Mrs. Dash® original blend s
  2 tb. unsalted tomato sauce
  1 c. finely chopped tomato, drain
    juice
  1 c. finely chopped onion
  1 c. finely chopped green peppe
  4 oz. part-skim mozzarella chee
  4 tb. reduced-fat and -calorie so
  2 oz. alfalfa sprouts, washed ar
    a paper towel
  4 9" flour tortillas
  8 toothpicks

For quick assembly, steam vegeta
cook beans ahead, mixing with sa

  1. Steam onions and peppers,
  2. In food processor, mix bean
seasoning.
  3. To assemble, spread each
mixture, tomatoes, peppers and
cheese, sour cream and sprouts
with 2 toothpicks.
  4. Spray 10" x 15" baking sh
coating. Bake in oven preheate
8 to 10 minutes or until heated
melts. Or heat on serving plate
cheese melts.

Hints for preparation: Include information on whether the dish can be prepared in advance, frozen and reheated, or doubled.

Suggestions
Serve with fresh fruit and vege

Suggestions: Hints on complementary dishes and appropriate garnishes.

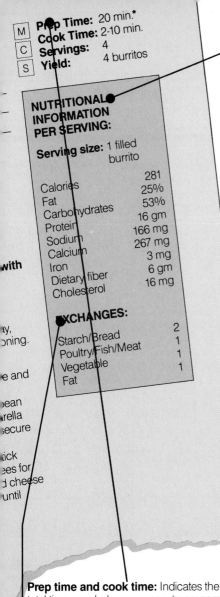

M
C
S

Prep Time: 20 min.*
Cook Time: 2-10 min.
Servings: 4
Yield: 4 burritos

NUTRITIONAL INFORMATION PER SERVING:

Serving size: 1 filled burrito

Calories	281
Fat	25%
Carbohydrates	53%
Protein	16 gm
Sodium	166 mg
Calcium	267 mg
Iron	3 mg
Dietary fiber	6 gm
Cholesterol	16 mg

EXCHANGES:

Starch/Bread	2
Poultry/Fish/Meat	1
Vegetable	1
Fat	1

with

ay,
oning.

e and

bean
arella
secure

kick
es for
d cheese
until

Prep time and cook time: Indicates the total time needed, on average, to prepare each recipe.

Exchanges: For individuals who are familiar with it, the food exchange system can simplify the task of planning a balanced diet. It enables individuals to easily determine approximate amounts of protein, carbohydrates, fat and total calories in individual foods, complete meals or daily menus, and to combine foods to achieve a desired balance. The exchange system divides food into six groups: starch/bread; poultry/fish/meat; vegetables; fruit; milk and fat.

Nutritional information: Indicates the amount of important dietary nutrients included in each serving. Nutritional information may vary, depending on the version of the recipe prepared; where versions vary significantly, additional information is provided.

Serving size: Portion control is important in a meal plan. Each recipe lists a serving size.

Calories: For the benefit of dieters and calorie counters, the number of calories per serving is listed.

% Fat: With few exceptions, the main and side dish recipes contain less than 30% fat; most are under 20% fat, in keeping with Dietary Guidelines for Americans and the American Heart Association's guidelines.

% Carbohydrates: This figure reflects an effort to maintain a high level of carbohydrates, particularly complex carbohydrates. These percentages are in keeping with current dietary guidelines.

Protein: Protein comes from both animal and plant sources. The protein level in each recipe has been calculated to reduce the amount of protein consumed to levels in accordance with nutritional guidelines.

Sodium, Calcium, Iron: Amounts of calcium and iron are provided to give dietary sources for these nutrients. The level of sodium, perhaps the most carefully tracked mineral, is well within safe guidelines in every case. With the exception of bread recipes, no salt has been added to any recipe; salt-free ingredients were used to further lower sodium. Flavoring was enhanced through the use of herbs and spices.

Cholesterol: Amounts are minimal, due to the conservative use of animal products—the source of cholesterol. All recipes fall within the accepted dietary guidelines.

Dietary fiber: Eating a variety of food high in fiber can be beneficial. Whole grains, fresh fruits and vegetables, rice and legumes are widely used in the recipes to maximize dietary fiber.

HOW TO USE YOUR COOKBOOK

Protein Complementation

Well-balanced diets must contain adequate amounts of protein. But what is protein?

Protein is comprised of individual units called amino acids. There are 22 different types of amino acids, nine of which must be supplied by our diet and are called essential amino acids. The others are produced in our bodies daily, as needed.

Foods from animal sources—such as milk, cheese, eggs, meat, fish and poultry—contain protein composed of all nine essential amino acids. But foods from plant sources—such as whole grains, nuts, seeds and legumes—contain protein that is missing one or more of the nine essential amino acids. By combining foods from different plant groups, all essential amino acids can be present in the combination. This is called protein complementation.

Below is a chart depicting some of the combinations that provide complete proteins (those containing all essential amino acids).

Examples of grain-legume combinations would be rice and lentils, rice and beans, pasta with a tofu-tomato sauce, bean-barley soup or a bean burrito.

Combinations of grains and seeds or nuts, such as rice with sesame seeds or bread with nuts or seeds, would do the same.

So would legume-seed/nut combinations. Examples are sunflower seeds and roasted soybeans, or hummus (a dip made from garbanzo beans and sesame paste).

As you can see, it takes some planning to ensure that meatless meals contain complete protein, but they aren't difficult to prepare. See Meatless Meals (page 57) for recipes that feature protein complementation.

Combine any one item from two of the three boxes to provide a complete protein.

GRAINS	
WHEAT	GRAIN PRODUCTS
OATS	—bread
CORN	—bagels
BARLEY	—muffins
MILLET	—pasta
BULGUR	
RICE	
RYE	

SEEDS/NUTS
SUNFLOWER SEEDS
SESAME SEEDS
PUMPKIN SEEDS
WALNUTS
PINE NUTS

LEGUMES (BEANS)
BEANS—lima, kidney, pinto, black, navy, mung beans
TOFU—soybeans
LENTILS   CHICK PEAS (garbanzo beans)

SOUPS & Sauces

Clockwise from bottom: Basic Tomato Sauce, Parsley-Orange Sauce, Hot or Cold Vegetable Soup, Cream of Asparagus Soup.

INDEX

Cream of Asparagus Soup   8
Cream of Potato Soup   9
Cabbage and Potato Soup   10
Potato-Rice Soup   11
Lentil-Rice Soup   12
Turkey-Lentil Soup   13
Thick and Hearty Bean-Barley Soup   14
Bean-Barley Chicken Soup   15
Hot or Cold Vegetable Soup   16
Cabbage Stew With Beef   17
Chili   18
Meatless Chili   19
Spaghetti Sauce With Beef   20
Meatless Spaghetti Sauce   21
Basic Tomato Sauce   22
Pizza Sauce   23
Basil-Orange Glaze   24
Parsley-Orange Sauce   24
Soy-Orange Sauce   25
Chunky Pineapple Sauce   25
Low-Sugar/Salt Basting or Barbeque Sauce   26
Healthy Topping   26

You could call soup the Versatile Meal. Whether you serve guests an elegant Cream of Asparagus Soup as a prelude to Salmon Filet with Dill Sauce, or pair a mug of hearty Cabbage and Potato Soup with Oat Bran Muffins for an easy weekend lunch, soup is simple to make, delicious and as good for you as food gets.

It's surprisingly efficient, too.

Throw together a few ingredients before you leave for work and your crockpot will have Lentil-Rice Soup ready when you get home. Or take frozen Basic Chicken Stock directly from the freezer and prepare Cabbage and Potato Soup in just an hour. Many of the following recipes can be frozen, doubled or prepared in a crockpot.

The recipes for cream soups are fat- and calorie-controlled, with skim milk, rather than cream, serving as the base.

Hints

- Refrigerate or freeze stock in pre-measured portions so it can be added without thawing.
- Freeze stock in ice cube trays, then transfer cubes to a freezer bag. Use in recipes calling for small amounts of stock, to stir-fry vegetables or to give flavor to sauces.

Basic Vegetable Stock

Clear or Pureed
Yield: 2 qts.

8 c. water
2 c. chopped onion
1 c. chopped carrots
1 c. celery
1 clove garlic
1 c. fresh parsley, stems trimmed

Combine ingredients and simmer for 45 minutes.

For clear stock: Strain liquid, discarding vegetables. Use or store.

For pureed stock: With a slotted spoon, remove vegetables. Puree in food processor or blender until smooth. Return to stock and blend. Use or store.

Basic Beef or Chicken Stock

Yield: 4 qts.

Several beef bones, meat trimmed
OR 2 chicken breasts, skin removed
OR 1 turkey neck, skin removed
5 qts. water
1 whole onion, peeled

Combine ingredients in *6-qt. stock pot.* Cover and simmer for 1½ hours. Remove bones and onion, discard. Chill stock overnight. Skim off any visible fat before using or freezing.

Soups and Sauces 7

B L D A/S T

M Prep Time: 20 min.
Cook Time: 40 min.
C Servings: 8
S Yield: 10 c.

CREAM OF ASPARAGUS SOUP

3 c. trimmed, chopped asparagus (15-18 spears)
2 c. chopped onion
1 medium potato, peeled and cubed
2 c. water
1 tsp. cilantro (dried coriander)
½ tsp. pepper
2 c. skim milk
2 tb. cornstarch
1 tb. parsley
1 c. nonfat yogurt
2 tb. margarine
1-3 tsp. fresh lemon juice
Steamed asparagus tips or thin lemon slices,
if desired

Recipe can be easily doubled and freezes well.
Prepare ahead and refrigerate.

1. In *3-qt. pot,* combine asparagus, onion, potato,
water, coriander and pepper. Cover and simmer until
vegetables are soft (about 40 minutes).
2. Meanwhile, over medium-high heat, stir together
cornstarch and milk in *6-qt stock pot.* Add margarine,
stirring constantly. Cook until mixture is thick and
bubbly. Remove from heat.
3. In food processor or blender, puree cooked
vegetables until smooth, making small batches. Blend
each batch into milk mixture, then add yogurt and
lemon juice. Reheat, if desired, and serve.

Suggestions
Serve hot or cold with Oat Bran Muffins (page 101) and
Delightful Fruit Salad (page 39). Or serve as a first
course. Garnish each bowl with thin lemon slices or
steamed asparagus tips.

NUTRITIONAL INFORMATION PER SERVING:

Serving size: 1¼ c.

Calories	117
Fat	25%
Carbohydrates	55%
Protein	6 gm
Sodium	92 mg
Calcium	165 mg
Iron	1 mg
Dietary fiber	2 gm
Cholesterol	2 mg

EXCHANGES:

Starch/Bread	⅓
Vegetable	1
Milk	½

CREAM OF POTATO SOUP

8 c. peeled, cubed potatoes (approx. 2½ lbs.)
4 c. skim milk
6 c. water
3 c. thinly sliced celery
3 c. thinly sliced onion
4 tb. cornstarch
2 tb. vegetable oil
1 tb. dill
1 tb. parsley
2 tsp. Mrs. Dash® lemon-and-herb seasoning
1 tsp. freshly ground pepper
2 c. diced carrots or broccoli, if desired
Dried or fresh parsley

Recipe can be made ahead and reheated. The longer it sits, the thicker it becomes. Freezes well.

1. In *6-qt. stock pot,* saute onion and celery in oil. Do not brown.

2. Meanwhile, peel and cube potatoes. In *6-c. measuring cup,* blend together milk and cornstarch. Add to onion mixture, along with potatoes and remaining ingredients. Stirring occasionally, simmer partially covered for 1 hour or until potatoes are soft. Mash potatoes slightly while in pot with a potato masher. Garnish with fresh or dried parsely, if desired. Serve or store.

Suggestions
Serve with warm bread and a large tossed salad with Vinaigrette Regular (page 42).

NUTRITIONAL INFORMATION PER SERVING:

Serving size: 1½ c.

Calories	194
Fat	15%
Carbohydrates	73%
Protein	6 gm
Sodium	91 mg
Calcium	163 mg
Iron	1 mg
Dietary fiber	2 gm
Cholesterol	2 mg

EXCHANGES:

Starch/Bread	1½
Vegetable	½
Milk	½
Fat	½

B ☐L☐ ☐D☐ A/S ☐T☐

CABBAGE AND POTATO SOUP
Crockpot Option

**8 c. Basic Beef or Chicken Stock (page 7) or
   Basic Vegetable Stock (page 7)**
4 c. water
**1 head cabbage (2 to 2¼ lbs.), cut into bite-sized
   pieces**
4 c. chopped onion
4 c. cubed potatoes (1¼ lbs.)
½ c. uncooked brown rice
1 clove garlic, chopped
2 tsp. basil
1 tsp. freshly ground pepper
1 tb. margarine

Recipe can be doubled and freezes well.

1. Combine all ingredients in *6-qt. stock pot* and bring to a boil. Reduce heat to low boil and cook covered ½ hour. Partially uncover and cook ½ hour longer or until potatoes and cabbage are soft. Serve or store.

Note: For Crockpot Option, cut recipe in half.

Suggestions
Serve with Crusty Continental Bread (page 108), and Pear-Gelatin Salad (page 41).

**NUTRITIONAL
INFORMATION
PER SERVING:**

Serving size: 1½ c.

Calories	161
Fat	9%
Carbohydrates	72%
Protein	8 gm
Sodium	60 mg
Calcium	83 mg
Iron	2 mg
Dietary fiber	5 gm
Cholesterol	0 mg

EXCHANGES:

Starch/Bread	1
Vegetable	2
Fat	Tr

B L D A/S T

M **Prep Time:** 15 min.
  Cook Time: 45 min.
C **Servings:** 8
S **Yield:** 12 c.

POTATO-RICE SOUP

10 c. Basic Vegetable Stock (page 7) or water
5 c. peeled, cubed potatoes (1¾ lbs.)
⅓ c. uncooked brown rice
½ c. diced carrot
1 tb. Mrs. Dash® lemon-and-herb seasoning
2 tb. vegetable oil
2 c. diced onion
1 tb. unbleached all-purpose flour
Freshly ground pepper

Recipe doubles easily and can be made ahead and
reheated. The longer it sits, the thicker it becomes.

1. In *6-qt. stock pot,* bring stock or water to a boil.
Add rice and cook covered for 15 minutes. Add
potatoes and carrots and cook partially covered 30
minutes more, stirring occasionally.

2. Meanwhile, in a *12" nonstick frying pan,* saute
onions in oil until soft but not brown. Add flour. Cook
and stir for 1 minute.

3. Pour onion mixture into soup, and stir in seasoning. Cook 10 minutes longer. Mash potatoes slightly
while in pot with a potato masher. Serve or store.

Suggestions
Serve with Cold Bean Salad (page 36) and whole-grain
rolls.

**NUTRITIONAL
INFORMATION
PER SERVING:**

Serving size: 1½ c.

Calories	170
Fat	20%
Carbohydrates	73%
Protein	3 gm
Sodium	10 mg
Calcium	23 mg
Iron	1 mg
Dietary fiber	3 gm
Cholesterol	0 mg

EXCHANGES:

Starch/Bread	1½
Vegetable	½
Fat	¾

B L D A/S T

LENTIL-RICE SOUP
Crockpot Option

2 16-oz. cans unsalted tomatoes, coarsely
  chopped
2 cloves garlic
2 c. chopped onion
1 c. lentils, rinsed and sorted
1½ c. chopped celery
6 c. water
1½ tsp. dill
4 tsp. vegetable oil
⅓ c. uncooked brown rice
1 tb. parsley
Freshly ground pepper
Lemon wedges, if desired

Recipe may be doubled and freezes well. Serve hot or
cold.

1. Combine all ingredients in a *4 to 6-qt. stock pot.*
Simmer partially covered 2 to 3 hours. Serve or store.

Suggestions
Serve with Oat Bran Muffins (page 101).

**NUTRITIONAL
INFORMATION
PER SERVING:**

Serving size: 1¾ c.

Calories	145
Fat	17%
Carbohydrates	66%
Protein	6 gm
Sodium	58 mg
Calcium	73 mg
Iron	2 mg
Dietary fiber	5 gm
Cholesterol	0 mg

EXCHANGES:

Starch/Bread	1¼
Vegetable	1
Fat	½

B L D A/S T

M
C
S

Prep Time: 20 min.
Cook Time: 4 hrs.
Servings: 14
Yield: 7 qts.

TURKEY-LENTIL SOUP

1 turkey drumstick, skinned (1¼ lbs.)
5 c. chopped onions
5 c. chopped celery
5 c. chopped carrots
1½ c. medium barley
2 c. lentils
1 c. chopped fresh parsley
1 tb. margarine
1 tb. fresh lemon juice
7 qts. water

Freezes well.

1. Combine all ingredients except ½ c. parsley in *10-qt. stock pot* and bring to a boil. Reduce heat and simmer, partially covered for 3 to 4 hours, stirring occasionally. Remove turkey bones and add reserved parsley 15 minutes before soup is done. Serve or store.

Suggestions
Serve with whole-grain rolls and a tossed salad with Yogurt-Poppyseed Dressing (page 43).

**NUTRITIONAL
INFORMATION
PER SERVING:**

Serving size: 2 c.

Calories	264
Fat	10%
Carbohydrates	65%
Protein	17 gm
Sodium	109 mg
Calcium	81 mg
Iron	4 mg
Dietary fiber	7 gm
Cholesterol	21 mg

EXCHANGES:

Starch/Bread	2
Poultry/Fish/Meat	1
Vegetable	1

B ☐L☐ ☐D☐ A/S ☐T☐

Prep Time: 20 min.
Cook Time: 3-4 hrs.
Servings: 15
☐S☐ **Yield:** 7½ qts.

THICK AND HEARTY BEAN-BARLEY SOUP

Crockpot Option. See Also
Bean-Barley Chicken Soup (page 15)

5 qts. Basic Vegetable Stock (page 7) or water
4 c. diced celery
4 c. diced carrots
2 c. dried pinto beans, rinsed and sorted
 OR 5 c. cooked beans
2 c. chopped onion
1½ c. whole-hulled barley
 OR 1½ c. medium barley
1⅓ c. uncooked brown rice
2-3 tb. Mrs. Dash® lemon-and-herb seasoning
1 tsp. pepper
3 tb. margarine
¾ c. chopped fresh parsley
 OR ½ c. dried parsley
Lemon wedges

Freezes well.

1. Combine all ingredients except lemon wedges in
8-qt. stock pot. Bring to a boil, reduce heat and
simmer partially covered for 3 to 4 hours, stirring
occasionally.

Note: For Crockpot Option, cut recipe in half.

Suggestions
Serve with lemon wedges, Crusty Continental Bread
(page 108) and Pear-Gelatin Salad (page 41).

Whole-hulled barley, which has a nutty taste, is
available in specialty shops, health food stores, and
some grocery stores.

**NUTRITIONAL
INFORMATION
PER SERVING:**

Serving size: 2 c.

Calories	247
Fat	12%
Carbohydrates	76%
Protein	8 gm
Sodium	84 mg
Calcium	61 mg
Iron	2 mg
Dietary fiber	8 gm
Cholesterol	0 mg

EXCHANGES:

Starch/Bread	2½
Vegetable	¾
Fat	½

14 *Menu for Life*

B ☐L☐ ☐D☐ A/S ☐T☐

M
C
S

Prep Time: 20 min.
Cook Time: 3-4 hrs.
Servings: 15
Yield: 5½ qts.

BEAN-BARLEY CHICKEN SOUP

Crockpot Option. See Also Thick and
Hearty Bean-Barley Soup (page 14)

4 qts. Basic Chicken Stock (page 7) or water
1 c. diced cooked chicken (4 oz. cooked weight),
OR 6 oz. uncooked boneless chicken breast,
diced
4 c. chopped celery
4 c. chopped carrots
2 c. dried pinto beans, rinsed and sorted
OR 5 c. cooked beans
2 c. chopped onion
1 c. whole-hulled barley
OR 1½ c. medium barley
3 tb. Mrs. Dash® lemon-and-herb seasoning
1 tsp. pepper
3 tb. margarine
¾ c. chopped fresh parsley
OR ½ c. dried parsley
Lemon wedges

Recipe freezes well.

1. Combine all ingredients except lemon wedges in
6 to 8-qt. stock pot. Cook partially covered on medium
to medium-high heat for 3 to 4 hours, stirring
occasionally.

Note: For Crockpot Option, cut recipe in half.

Suggestions
Serve with lemon wedges, Crusty Continental Bread
(page 108) and Pear-Gelatin Salad (page 41).

Whole-hulled barley, which has a nutty taste, is
available at specialty shops, health food stores and
some grocery stores.

NUTRITIONAL INFORMATION PER SERVING:

Serving size: 1½ c.

Calories	214
Fat	13%
Carbohydrates	60%
Protein	14 gm
Sodium	131 mg
Calcium	70 mg
Iron	3 mg
Dietary fiber	7 gm
Cholesterol	6 mg

EXCHANGES:

Starch/Bread	1½
Poultry/Fish/Meat	¼
Vegetable	1
Fat	½

B ☐L☐ ☐D☐ A/S ☐T☐

M **Prep Time:** 20 min.
  Cook Time: 3 hrs.
C **Servings:** 16
S **Yield:** 6 qts. soup
           8 c. pasta

HOT OR COLD VEGETABLE SOUP
Crockpot Option

2 c. chopped celery
2 c. chopped bell pepper
4 c. chopped broccoli (reserve florets)
8 c. chopped tomatoes, canned or fresh
2½ c. dried garbanzo beans, rinsed and sorted
        OR 6¼ c. cooked garbanzo beans
2½ c. dried pinto beans, rinsed and sorted
        OR 6¼ c. cooked pinto beans
4 c. chopped onions
6-oz. can unsalted tomato paste
1 tsp. chili powder (or to taste)
1 tsp. freshly ground pepper
1 tb. cilantro (dried coriander)
3 tb. vegetable oil
12 c. water (8-10 c. if using cooked beans)
4 c. small pasta, uncooked
Lemon wedges

NUTRITIONAL INFORMATION PER SERVING:

Serving size:
1½ c. soup, ½ c. pasta

Calories	330
Fat	16%
Carbohydrates	67%
Protein	15 gm
Sodium	49 mg
Calcium	119 mg
Iron	5 mg
Dietary fiber	3 gm
Cholesterol	0 mg

EXCHANGES:

Starch/Bread	3
Vegetable	1½
Fat	½

Freezes well. If using canned tomatoes, use liquid and reduce water by an equal amount.

1. Combine all ingredients except pasta and lemon wedges in *8-qt. stock pot.* Cover and bring to a boil. Reduce heat and simmer partially covered, stirring occasionally, for 2-3 hours. If using uncooked beans, allow 3 hours cooking time.

2. In *3-qt. saucepan,* cook pasta according to package directions, one-half hour before soup is done. Meanwhile, add broccoli florets to soup. To serve, place ½ c. cooked pasta in serving bowl, top with soup and stir gently. Serve.

Note: For Crockpot Option, cut recipe in half.

Suggestions
Serve hot or cold with Crusty Continental Bread (page 108) and lemon wedges. Bake bread while soup is cooking. Soup is delicious chilled and served directly from the refrigerator on a hot day.

CABBAGE STEW WITH BEEF
Crockpot Option

**8 oz. lean sirloin (fat trimmed), thinly sliced into
     bite-sized pieces**
4 c. sliced celery
3 c. sliced onion
2 lb. head of cabbage, cut into bite-sized pieces
**3 16-oz. cans unsalted tomatoes, coarsely
     chopped**
4 c. peeled, cubed potatoes (1¼ lb.)
2 cloves garlic, diced
¼ c. unbleached, all-purpose flour
1 c. water
½ tsp. freshly ground pepper
1 tsp. cilantro (dried coriander)
1 tb. vegetable oil

Freezes well.

   1. Spray *8-qt. stock pot* with nonstick coating, add
oil and heat on medium high.
   2. Brown meat lightly in oil.
   3. Blend in remaining ingredients (except flour
and water) and continue cooking for 30 minutes,
stirring occasionally.
   4. Remove lid, mix together flour and water, stir into
stew. Reduce heat to medium and continue cooking
partially covered for 30 minutes longer or until potatoes
and cabbage are soft. Serve immediately or store.

Note: For Crockpot Option, cut recipe in half.

Suggestions
Serve with muffins and Delightful Fruit Salad (page 39).

**NUTRITIONAL
INFORMATION
PER SERVING:**

Serving size: 2 c.

Calories	192
Fat	17%
Carbohydrates	64%
Protein	10 gm
Sodium	101 mg
Calcium	79 mg
Iron	4 mg
Dietary fiber	5 gm
Cholesterol	15 mg

EXCHANGES:

Starch/Bread	1
Poultry/Fish/Meat	½
Vegetable	2
Fat	⅓

B ☐ L ☐ D ☐ A/S ☐ T

M **Prep Time:** 20 min.
C **Cook Time:** 3-4 hrs.
Servings: 18
S **Yield:** 6¾ qts.

CHILI
Crockpot Option
See Also Meatless Chili (page 19)

6 c. Basic Beef or Chicken Stock (page 7)
or water
6 oz. beef sirloin (fat trimmed), diced
6 oz. chicken breast, skinned, diced and boned
2 c. chopped celery
4 c. chopped onion
3 cloves garlic, chopped
8 c. chopped unsalted tomatoes, canned, fresh
or frozen
2¼ c. dried kidney beans, rinsed and sorted
OR 5½ c. cooked kidney beans
2¼ c. dried pinto beans, rinsed and sorted
OR 5½ c. cooked pinto beans
⅔ c. chopped fresh parsley
¼ c. unsalted tomato paste
1-3 tsp. chili powder
1 tsp. pepper
4 c. water

Recipe freezes well and can be doubled in a *10 to 12-qt. stock pot.*

1. Combine all ingredients in *8-qt. stock pot.*
Bring to a boil. Reduce to medium heat and cook
partially covered for 3 to 4 hours, stirring occasionally.
Serve immediately or store.

Note: For Crockpot Option, cut recipe in half.

Suggestions
Serve with warm muffins and Pear-Gelatin Salad
(page 41).

NUTRITIONAL INFORMATION PER SERVING:	
Serving size: 1½ c.	
Calories	210
Fat	7%
Carbohydrates	63%
Protein	16 gm
Sodium	60 mg
Calcium	68 mg
Iron	5 mg
Dietary fiber	10 gm
Cholesterol	11 mg

EXCHANGES:	
Starch/Bread	1½
Poultry/Fish/Meat	½
Vegetable	1
Fat	½

B L ☐ D A/S ☐ T

MEATLESS CHILI
Crockpot Option
See Also Chili With Meat (page 18)

2 c. chopped celery
4 c. chopped onion
3 cloves garlic, chopped
8 c. unsalted tomatoes, canned, fresh or frozen
2½ c. dried kidney beans, rinsed and sorted
      OR 6¼ c. cooked kidney beans
2½ c. dried pinto beans, rinsed and sorted
      OR 6¼ c. cooked pinto beans
1 c. chopped fresh parsley
¼ c. unsalted tomato paste
1 tb. vegetable oil
1-3 tsp. chili powder
1 tsp. pepper
10 c. water
3 c. uncooked brown rice

Recipe freezes well.

1. Combine all ingredients except rice in *8-qt. stock pot.* Bring to a boil. Reduce to medium heat and cook partially covered for 3 to 3½ hours, stirring occasionally.
2. Meanwhile, cook rice in *3-qt. sauce pot* according to package directions. Set aside.
3. To serve, place ½ c. rice in serving bowl and top with 1½ c. chili.

Note: For Crockpot Option, cut recipe in half.

Suggestions
Serve with bread and a gelatin salad.

NUTRITIONAL INFORMATION PER SERVING:	
Serving size: 1½ c. chili	
½ c. rice	
Calories	299
Fat	6%
Carbohydrates	77%
Protein	13 gm
Sodium	40 mg
Calcium	77 mg
Iron	6 mg
Dietary fiber	13 gm
Cholesterol	0 mg
EXCHANGES:	
Starch/Bread	3½
Vegetable	1

B L D A/S T

M **Prep Time:** 20 min.
Cook Time: 3½ hrs.
C **Servings:** 16
S **Yield:** 4 qts.

SPAGHETTI SAUCE WITH BEEF

See Also Meatless Spaghetti Sauce
(page 21)

1 lb. extra lean ground beef or thinly sliced sirloin
 (fat trimmed)
6 large onions, chopped (2¼ lbs.)
6 cloves garlic, chopped
2 18-oz. cans unsalted tomato paste
2 28-oz. cans unsalted tomatoes, coarsely
 chopped
12 c. Basic Chicken or Beef Stock (page 7)
 or water or combination
1 tb. vegetable oil
½ tsp. pepper
1 tb. parsley
1 tb. oregano
2 tb. basil

Recipe freezes well. If doubled, use a *12-qt. stock pot.*

1. Combine and heat meat, onions, garlic and
tomato paste in *8-qt. stock pot,* stirring to blend in
paste and to break up meat. Add remaining ingredients, blending well. Bring to a medium-low boil and
cook partially covered for 2 hours, stirring occasionally.
Remove lid and cook for another 1½ to 2 hours, continuing to stir occasionally.
 2. Remove from heat. Serve immediately or store.

Suggestions
Serve over cooked pasta, with warm bread and a large
tossed salad with Vinaigrette (page 42).

NUTRITIONAL INFORMATION PER SERVING:	
Serving size: 1 c.	
Calories	167
Fat	22%
Carbohydrates	53%
Protein	11 gm
Sodium	83 mg
Calcium	91 mg
Iron	4 mg
Dietary fiber	2 gm
Cholesterol	19 mg

EXCHANGES:	
Poultry/Fish/Meat	1
Vegetable	3½
Fat	½

MEATLESS SPAGHETTI SAUCE

Tomato or Tofu. See Also Spaghetti Sauce
With Beef (page 20)

TOMATO SPAGHETTI SAUCE

6 c. chopped onions
6 garlic cloves, chopped
2 18-oz. cans unsalted tomato paste
2 28-oz. cans unsalted tomatoes, coarsely
    chopped
12 c. Basic Vegetable Stock, clear or pureed
    (page 7), or water or combination
2 tb. vegetable oil
3 4-oz. cans mushroom pieces, drained
½ tsp. pepper
1 tb. parsley
1 tb. oregano
1 tb. basil

TOFU SPAGHETTI SAUCE

Above ingredients, plus
1 lb. regular curd tofu, pureed in food processor

Recipe freezes well. If doubled, use a *12-qt. stock pot.*

TOMATO SPAGHETTI SAUCE

1. Blend together tomato paste and chopped
tomatoes in *8-qt. stock pot.* Stir in remaining
ingredients.
2. Bring to a boil. Reduce heat to a medium-low boil
and cook partially covered for 1 hour, stirring occasionally. Remove lid; cook 2 hours more, continuing to
stir occasionally.
3. Remove from heat. Use or store.

TOFU SPAGHETTI SAUCE

Follow above steps, adding tofu ½ hour before sauce
is done. This sauce will be lighter in color than tomato
sauce. Freezes well.

Suggestions
Serve with pasta, Crusty Continental Bread (page 108)
and Cold Bean Salad (page 36).

**NUTRITIONAL
INFORMATION
PER SERVING:**

Tomato Spaghetti Sauce

Serving size: 1 c.

Calories	129
Fat	16%
Carbohydrates	70%
Protein	5 gm
Sodium	67 mg
Calcium	55 mg
Iron	5 mg
Dietary fiber	1 gm
Cholesterol	0 mg

EXCHANGES:

Vegetable	3½
Fat	½

Tofu Spaghetti Sauce:

Serving size: 1 c.

Calories	150
Fat	20%
Carbohydrates	62%
Protein	7 gm
Sodium	69 mg
Calcium	91 mg
Iron	5 mg
Dietary fiber	1 gm
Cholesterol	0 mg

EXCHANGES:

Poultry/Fish/Meat	½
Vegetable	3½
Fat	1

M   **Prep Time:** 10 min.
C   **Cook Time:** 1 hr.
    Servings: 5
S   **Yield:** 3⅓ c.

BASIC TOMATO SAUCE

1 15-oz. can unsalted tomato sauce
1 15-oz. can unsalted tomatoes, coarsely chopped
1 bay leaf
1 c. chopped onion
1 clove garlic, finely chopped
1 c. water
1 tsp. basil
½ tsp. thyme
½ tsp. allspice

Recipe can be doubled. Freezes well or will keep in
refrigerator in an air-tight container for up to 1 week.

   1. Combine all ingredients in *2-qt. stock pot.* Bring
to a low boil and cook covered for 15 minutes.
   2. Remove lid and simmer for 45 minutes, stirring
occasionally. Remove from heat, serve or store.
   3. Cook longer to thicken sauce.

Suggestions
Serve over rice or noodles, meat, chicken or fish.

**NUTRITIONAL
INFORMATION
PER SERVING:**

Serving size: ⅔ c.

Calories	67
Fat	2%
Carbohydrates	82%
Protein	3 gm
Sodium	16 mg
Calcium	20 mg
Iron	2 mg
Dietary fiber	1 gm
Cholesterol	0 mg

EXCHANGES:

Vegetable	2½

B L D A/S T

PIZZA SAUCE

3 15-oz. cans unsalted tomato sauce
1 c. diced onions
3 cloves garlic, finely chopped
1 tb. basil
2 tsp. oregano
1 tb. vegetable oil

Makes enough sauce for 2 10″ x 15″ pizzas.

1. Combine all ingredients in *2-qt. stockpot.* Bring to a boil. Reduce heat to medium boil, and cook for 10 minutes. Remove lid, reduce heat and simmer for 50 minutes, stirring occasionally.

Suggestions
For a fast meal, split a loaf of Crusty Continental Bread (page 108), top with desired amount of Pizza Sauce and part-skim mozzarella cheese. Broil. Or use on Pizza (page 109).

NUTRITIONAL INFORMATION PER SERVING:

Serving size: 2½ tb.

Calories	24
Fat	18%
Carbohydrates	67%
Protein	1 gm
Sodium	0 mg
Calcium	7 mg
Iron	0 mg
Dietary fiber	0 gm
Cholesterol	0 mg

EXCHANGES:

Vegetable	½
Fat	Tr

B L D A/S T

BASIL-ORANGE GLAZE

½ c. orange juice
¼ c. orange conserve
2 tsp. cornstarch
2 tsp. basil

Recipe can be doubled, made ahead and refrigerated for up to 5 days. Freezes well.

1. In small saucepan, blend together orange juice and cornstarch. Cook and stir until thick and bubbly. Remove from heat. Stir in basil and orange conserve until well-blended. Serve or store.

Suggestions
Used as a glaze for fish or poultry. Or serve on the side as a condiment.

NUTRITIONAL INFORMATION PER SERVING:

Serving size: 2 tb.

Calories	42
Fat	2%
Carbohydrates	94%
Protein	0 gm
Sodium	0 mg
Calcium	12 mg
Iron	0 mg
Dietary fiber	0 gm
Cholesterol	0 mg

EXCHANGES:

Starch/Bread	⅛
Fruit	½

B L D A/S T

PARSLEY-ORANGE SAUCE

1 c. orange juice
½ c. dry white wine
4 tsp. cornstarch
1½ tsp. margarine
2 tsp. parsley

Recipe doubles easily and freezes well. It will keep refrigerated for up to 5 days.

1. In *1-qt. sauce pot,* blend together orange juice, wine and cornstarch. Heat, stirring frequently, until thick and bubbly. Cook 2 minutes longer.
2. Remove from heat, stir in remaining ingredients and serve immediately or store.

Suggestions
Use to baste chicken or fish or as a glaze after baking.

NUTRITIONAL INFORMATION PER SERVING:

Serving size: ¼ c.
(1 tb.=9 calories)

Calories	37
Fat	25%
Carbohydrates	63%
Protein	0 gm
Sodium	12 mg
Calcium	7 mg
Iron	0 mg
Dietary fiber	0 gm
Cholesterol	0 mg

EXCHANGES:

Starch/Bread	⅕
Fruit	⅓
Fat	Tr

B L D A/S T

M **Prep Time:** 2 min.
   Cook Time: 3 min.
C **Servings:** 4
S **Yield:** ½ c.

SOY-ORANGE SAUCE

6 tb. orange juice
2 tsp. vegetable oil
2 tsp. low-sodium soy sauce
2 tsp. cornstarch

Recipe doubles easily and will keep refrigerated for up to 5 days.

1. In small saucepan, combine above ingredients. Heat, stirring frequently, until thick and bubbly. Remove, serve or store.

Suggestions
Baste poultry or fish with sauce while baking, grilling or broiling. Or serve on the side as a condiment.

NUTRITIONAL INFORMATION PER SERVING:

Serving size: 2 tb.

Calories	35
Fat	58%
Carbohydrates	40%
Protein	0 gm
Sodium	91 mg
Calcium	3 mg
Iron	0 mg
Dietary fiber	0 gm
Cholesterol	0 mg

EXCHANGES:

Starch/Bread	⅛
Fruit	¼
Fat	⅛

B L D A/S T

M **Prep Time:** 15 min.
   Cook Time: 20 min.
C **Servings:** 12
S **Yield:** 4 c.

CHUNKY PINEAPPLE SAUCE

6 c. peeled, sliced cooking apples (2¼ lb.)
1¼ c. crushed pineapple in unsweetened
       pineapple juice
1 tsp. lemon juice
1 tsp. cinnamon

Recipe can be easily doubled, made ahead and refrigerated for up to one week. Reheat if warm sauce is desired. If preferred, slice but do not peel apples and increase cooking time by 10 minutes.

1. Combine apples, pineapple, pineapple juice and lemon juice in *3-qt. saucepot.* Cover and cook on low boil for 20 minutes or until apples are soft. Remove from heat, mash slightly with the back of a spoon or potato masher. Blend in cinnamon and serve or store.

Suggestions
Serve with poultry, fish or meat dishes. Spread on toast or muffins, or mix with nonfat yogurt.

NUTRITIONAL INFORMATION PER SERVING:

Serving size: ⅓ c.
(1 tb.= 11 calories)

Calories	60
Fat	4%
Carbohydrates	95%
Protein	0 gm
Sodium	1 mg
Calcium	8 mg
Iron	0 mg
Dietary fiber	2 gm
Cholesterol	0 mg

EXCHANGES:

Fruit	1

B [L] [D] A/S T

M	**Prep Time:** 15 min.
C	**Cook Time:** none
	Servings: 16
S	**Yield:** 4 c.

LOW-SUGAR/SALT BASTING OR BARBEQUE SAUCE
For Poultry, Fish And Beef

16-oz. can unsalted tomatoes
6-oz. can unsalted tomato paste
2 cloves garlic
1¾ c. chopped onion
¼ c. cider vinegar
¾ c. orange, peach or pineapple conserve
2 tb. vegetable oil
1-2 tb. Mrs. Dash® extra spicy seasoning

Store in refrigerator. Freezes well.

1. In blender, combine all ingredients and mix until smooth. Store in covered container (glass jar with lid) in refrigerator.

Suggestions
Baste poultry, fish or meat with sauce while baking, broiling or grilling.

NUTRITIONAL INFORMATION PER SERVING:

Serving size: ¼ c.
(1 tb.= 19 calories)

Calories	74
Fat	29%
Carbohydrates	64%
Protein	1 gm
Sodium	104 mg
Calcium	10 mg
Iron	1 mg
Dietary fiber	0 gm
Cholesterol	0 mg

EXCHANGES:

Vegetable	¾
Fruit	½
Fat	½

B [L] [D] A/S T

M	**Prep Time:** 3 min.
C	**Cook Time:** none
	Servings: 8
S	**Yield:** ½ c.

HEALTHY TOPPING
A Sour Cream Substitute

½ c. ½%-fat cottage cheese
1 tb. ½%-fat buttermilk
Dill, basil, oregano, chives, parsley or herb of choice

1. In food processor, puree cottage cheese for 3 to 4 minutes, scraping sides frequently, or until it is the consistency of sour cream.
2. Add buttermilk and ½ tsp. herb (more if desired). Puree again.
3. Refrigerate in a covered container.

Suggestions
Prepare with favorite herb and use as a topping for baked potatoes, vegetables or fish. Spread on whole-grain bread and broil as a snack or light meal. Thin with buttermilk to desired consistency and serve as a dip.

NUTRITIONAL INFORMATION PER SERVING:

Serving size: 1 tb.

Calories	9
Fat	6%
Carbohydrates	14%
Protein	2 gm
Sodium	3 mg
Calcium	5 mg
Iron	0 mg
Dietary fiber	0 gm
Cholesterol	1 mg

EXCHANGES:

Poultry/Fish/Meat	⅕

SALADS & *Dressings*

Clockwise from bottom: Chilled Orange-Rice Salad (with shrimp), Yogurt-Poppyseed Dressing, Select a Salad, Hot Pasta Salad, Strawberry-Banana Salad.

INDEX

Salad That's A Meal   30
Potato Salad   31
Vegetable-Pasta Salad   32
Hot Pasta Salad   33
Variable Pasta Salad   34
Cold Bean Salad   36
Overnight Rice and Bean Salad   37
Chilled Orange-Rice Salad   38
Delightful Fruit Salad   39
Strawberry-Banana Salad   40
Pear-Gelatin Salad   41
Soy Vinaigrette   41
Vinaigrette   42
Yogurt-Poppyseed Dressing   43
Yogurt-Dijon Dressing   43
Orange-Yogurt Dressing   44
Lemon-Orange Dressing   44
Chicken or Fish Marinade   45
Vegetable Marinade   45
Fruit Dressing   46

T here's a lot more to salad than plain old lettuce. Unleash your creativity! Toss in apple slices or walnuts. Sprinkle with a dash of wheat germ for some extra fiber. Combine cooked potatoes and fresh spinach for Salad That's A Meal. The opportunities are limited only by your imagination.

Here's a great place to start the gears turning. Choose one ingredient from each column. Toss and serve with the salad dressing of your choice. Any combination has about 110-130 calories (before dressing).

Select a salad:

Lettuce	**Onion**
(3 c. torn)	(¼ c. sliced)
Romaine	Green onion
Spinach	Red onion
Bibb	Spanish onion
Iceberg	
Endive	

Fruit	**Crunch**
(½ med. sliced)	
Orange	1 tb. sunflower
Apple	seeds
¼ c. sliced	2 whole walnuts
Dried apricots	6 whole
	almonds
	1 tb. pine nuts
	½ c. croutons

Hints

- Potatoes can be boiled in the skin or cooked in a microwave oven, cooled, wrapped and refrigerated. They will keep for several days. Prepare recipe when convenient.
- Mash ripe bananas with a fork, or puree in food processor or blender. Freeze in premeasured portions. Use as directed in gelatin salads.

Low-calorie Mayonnaise Blend

Use instead of regular mayonnaise on bread and in making sandwich spreads.

¼ c. nonfat yogurt
1 tb. low-fat mayonnaise
2 tsp. herb or mustard of choice

Blend well with a fork. Refrigerate in air-tight container.

B ☐L☐ ☐D☐ A/S ☐T☐

M **Prep Time:** 10 min.*
Cook Time: none
C **Servings:** 2
S **Yield:** 8 c.

SALAD THAT'S A MEAL

*2 medium potatoes, boiled in the skin
   (4 oz. each)
*2 hard-boiled eggs whites
 6 c. fresh spinach, bibb or romaine lettuce
 ½ c. red onion, sliced thin
 1 medium unskinned apple, sliced
   OR 1 medium orange, peeled and sectioned
 1 tb. sunflower seeds
   OR 2 whole walnuts, broken

1. Combine ingredients and toss with dressing
of choice.

Suggestions
Serve with Oat Bran Muffins (page 101).

**NUTRITIONAL
INFORMATION
PER SERVING:**

Spinach Salad
(dressing not included)

Serving size: 4 c.

Calories	257
Fat	11%
Carbohydrates	72%
Protein	12 gm
Sodium	189 mg
Calcium	202 mg
Iron	6 mg
Dietary fiber	10 gm
Cholesterol	0 mg

EXCHANGES:

Starch/Bread	1½
Poultry/Fish/Meat	½
Vegetable	2
Fruit	1
Fat	½

Bibb or Romaine Salad
(dressing not included)

Serving size: 4 c.

Calories	245
Fat	11%
Carbohydrates	74%
Protein	10 gm
Sodium	69 mg
Calcium	94 mg
Iron	3 mg
Dietary fiber	7 gm
Cholesterol	0 mg

EXCHANGES:

Starch/Bread	1½
Poultry/Fish/Meat	½
Vegetable	1½
Fruit	1
Fat	½

M **Prep Time:** 15 min.*
C **Cook Time:** none
Servings: 6
S **Yield:** 7½ c.

POTATO SALAD
With Eggs or Beans

***6 medium potatoes, boiled, peeled and cubed
(about 1½ lbs.)**
***6 hard-boiled eggs, discard yolks
OR 1⅓ c. cooked kidney beans**
½ c. chopped mild red or green onion
1 c. finely chopped celery
5 tb. reduced-calorie and -fat mayonnaise
1 tb. Dijon-style mustard
½ c. nonfat yogurt
½ tsp. celery seed

1. Combine potatoes, onions, egg whites or beans
and celery in medium-size refrigerator bowl.
2. In small bowl, mix remaining ingredients with a
fork until well-blended. Pour over potato mixture and
toss to coat. Cover and chill before serving.

Suggestions
Goes well with McHealthy Chicken Nuggets (page 85),
Baked Chicken (page 79), or other main dishes. Serve
with rolls and fresh vegetable sticks or Marinated
Vegetables (page 56).

**NUTRITIONAL
INFORMATION
PER SERVING:**

Potato Salad With Eggs

Serving size: 1¼ c.

Calories	173
Fat	19%
Carbohydrates	65%
Protein	7 gm
Sodium	122 mg
Calcium	63 mg
Iron	0 mg
Dietary fiber	2 gm
Cholesterol	5 mg

EXCHANGES:

Starch/Bread	1¼
Poultry/Fish/Meat	½
Fat	1

Potato Salad With Beans

Serving size: 1⅓ c.

Calories	202
Fat	17%
Carbohydrates	70%
Protein	7 gm
Sodium	73 mg
Calcium	73 mg
Iron	2 mg
Dietary fiber	5 gm
Cholesterol	5 mg

EXCHANGES:

Starch/Bread	2
Fat	1

B L D A/S T

VEGETABLE-PASTA SALAD

1 c. chopped tomatoes
½ c. sliced fresh mushrooms
½ c. sliced green pepper
½ c. small vegetable pasta shells
½ medium apple, sliced
1 shelled walnut, broken
1 oz. part-skim mozzarella cheese, diced
1 recipe Orange-Yogurt Dressing (page 44)

Recipe doubles easily and can be made ahead.

1. Cook pasta according to package directions. Rinse and drain.
2. In medium bowl, combine macaroni and salad ingredients.
3. Prepare Orange-Yogurt Dressing, if not on hand.
4. Toss salad with dressing and serve.

Suggestions
Serve with warm bread and apple slices.

NUTRITIONAL INFORMATION PER SERVING:

Serving size: 3 c.

Calories	348
Fat	18%
Carbohydrates	63%
Protein	17 gm
Sodium	182 mg
Calcium	309 mg
Iron	3 mg
Dietary fiber	7 gm
Cholesterol	17 mg

EXCHANGES:

Starch/Bread	1½
Poultry/Fish/Meat	1
Vegetable	2
Fruit	1
Milk	Tr
Fat	1

B L D A/S T

M **Prep Time:** 10-15 min.*
Cook Time: 15 min.
C **Servings:** 4
S **Yield:** 5 c.

HOT PASTA SALAD
Cheese Or Bean

3 c. vegetable pasta shells
1 tb. olive oil
1½ c. thinly sliced onion
2 cloves garlic, diced
2 c. diced fresh or canned unsalted tomatoes
***1⅓ c. cooked garbanzo beans**
         OR 2 tb. grated parmesan cheese
1 tsp. basil

Recipe can be made ahead and reheated. It doubles easily, but use a wok to accommodate larger volume.

1. Cook pasta shells according to package directions.
2. Meanwhile, heat oil in *12" nonstick frying pan.* Saute onions and garlic in oil. When onions are soft, add tomatoes and basil.
3. Stir in drained, cooked pasta. Add beans or cheese, toss to coat. Serve or refrigerate.

Note: Together, beans and pasta provide a complemented protein.

Suggestions
Serve with Crusty Continental Bread (page 108) and sliced fresh fruit.

NUTRITIONAL INFORMATION PER SERVING:

Hot Pasta Salad With Beans

Serving size: 1⅔ c.

Calories	299
Fat	14%
Carbohydrates	72%
Protein	10 gm
Sodium	236 mg
Calcium	66 mg
Iron	4 mg
Dietary fiber	7 gm
Cholesterol	0 mg

EXCHANGES:

Starch/Bread	3
Vegetable	1½
Fat	½

Hot Pasta Salad With Cheese

Serving size: 1¼ c.

Calories	258
Fat	16%
Carbohydrates	70%
Protein	9 gm
Sodium	68 mg
Calcium	87 mg
Iron	2 mg
Dietary fiber	4 gm
Cholesterol	2 mg

EXCHANGES:

Starch/Bread	2½
Vegetable	1½
Fat	½

B ☐L☐ ☐D☐ A/S ☐T☐

Prep Time: 20 min.
C Cook Time: 10 min.
Servings: 4
☐S☐ Yield: 8 c.

VARIABLE PASTA SALAD
With Chicken, Tuna, Salmon or Shrimp

CHICKEN PASTA SALAD

1 c. diced cooked chicken
1½ c. vegetable macaroni or small pasta shells
2 oz. pimento, drained and chopped
¼ c. finely chopped green onion
1½ c. finely chopped celery
1 8-oz. can water chestnuts, drained and thinly
    sliced
2 c. frozen peas

Dressing

1 tb. orange or pineapple conserve
2 tsp. low-sodium soy sauce
2 tb. wine vinegar
2 tb. lemon juice
1 tb. vegetable oil
1 tb. low-fat mayonnaise
1 tb. water
Freshly ground pepper, to taste

TUNA PASTA SALAD

1 6½-oz. can water-packed tuna,
    drained and flaked
All ingredients above (omit chicken)

Recipe should be made at least 3 hours before
serving. Doubles easily.

1. Cook macaroni according to package directions.
Drain and turn in to medium-large bowl.
2. In small bowl, cover frozen peas with hot water
and let stand 2 minutes. Drain, add to noodles.
3. Add remaining salad ingredients.
4. In small container, mix salad dressing ingredients
with fork until well-blended. Pour over salad and toss.
Cover and refrigerate.

Suggestions
Serve with sliced, fresh tomatoes, whole-grain bread
and lemon wedges.

NUTRITIONAL INFORMATION PER SERVING:

Chicken Pasta Salad

Serving size: 2 c.

Calories	352
Fat	17%
Carbohydrates	61%
Protein	19 gm
Sodium	228 mg
Calcium	57 mg
Iron	3 mg
Dietary fiber	4 gm
Cholesterol	25 mg

EXCHANGES:

Starch/Bread	2¾
Poultry/Fish/Meat	1
Vegetable	1½
Fat	1

Tuna Pasta Salad

Serving size: 2 c.

Calories	364
Fat	16%
Carbohydrates	59%
Protein	23 gm
Sodium	374 mg
Calcium	56 mg
Iron	4 mg
Dietary fiber	4 gm
Cholesterol	17 mg

EXCHANGES:

Starch/Bread	2¾
Poultry/Fish/Meat	1
Vegetable	1½
Fat	1

B ☐L☐ ☐D☐ A/S ☐T☐

M Prep Time: 20 min.
C Cook Time: 10 min.
Servings: 4
S Yield: 8 c.

VARIABLE PASTA SALAD
Continued

SALMON PASTA SALAD

1 6½-oz. can water-packed salmon, drained and flaked

All above ingredients (omit chicken and tuna)

SHRIMP PASTA SALAD

1 c. diced cooked shrimp

All above ingredients (omit chicken, tuna and salmon)

Recipe should be made at least 3 hours before serving. Doubles easily.

1. Cook macaroni according to package directions. Drain and turn in to medium-large bowl.

2. In small bowl, cover frozen peas with hot water and let stand 2 minutes. Drain, add to noodles.

3. Add remaining salad ingredients.

4. In small container, mix salad dressing ingredients with fork until well-blended. Pour over salad and toss. Cover and refrigerate.

Suggestions
Serve with sliced, fresh tomatoes, whole-grain bread and lemon wedges.

NUTRITIONAL INFORMATION PER SERVING:

Salmon Pasta Salad

Serving size: 2 c.

Calories	370
Fat	20%
Carbohydrates	58%
Protein	20 gm
Sodium	446 mg
Calcium	143 mg
Iron	3 mg
Dietary fiber	4 gm
Cholesterol	20 mg

EXCHANGES:

Starch/Bread	2¾
Poultry/Fish/Meat	1
Vegetable	1½
Fat	1

Shrimp Pasta Salad

Serving size: 2 c.

Calories	344
Fat	15%
Carbohydrates	63%
Protein	18 gm
Sodium	267 mg
Calcium	79 mg
Iron	4 mg
Dietary fiber	4 gm
Cholesterol	62 mg

EXCHANGES:

Starch/Bread	2½
Poultry/Fish/Meat	1
Vegetable	1½
Fat	1½

B [L] [D] A/S [T]

COLD BEAN SALAD

*2½ c. cooked garbanzo beans
*1¼ c. cooked kidney beans
*1¼ c. cooked pinto beans
 ¾ c. thinly sliced red onion
 ½ c. frozen peas
 2 cloves garlic, diced
 2 tb. vegetable oil
 3 tb. lemon juice
 2 tb. frozen orange juice concentrate
 1 tb. wine vinegar
 Freshly ground pepper, to taste

1. In small bowl, cover frozen peas with hot water and let stand 2 minutes. Drain.

2. In large bowl, combine peas, beans, onions and garlic.

3. Mix well dressing ingredients. Pour over bean mixture and toss. Chill. The flavor will continue to improve during refrigeration.

Suggestions
Serve with warm bread or a pasta entree to complete the protein.

NUTRITIONAL INFORMATION PER SERVING:

Serving size: ½ c.

Calories	119
Fat	22%
Carbohydrates	60%
Protein	5 gm
Sodium	120 mg
Calcium	36 mg
Iron	2 mg
Dietary fiber	5 gm
Cholesterol	0 mg

EXCHANGES:

Starch/Bread	1
Vegetable	½
Fat	½

B L D A/S T

M **Prep Time:** 10-15 min.*
C **Cook Time:** none
  Servings: 4
S **Yield:** 5 c.

OVERNIGHT RICE & BEAN SALAD

*1 c. cooked kidney, garbanzo or pinto beans
*1½ c. cooked brown rice or Basic Rice (page 67)
¼ c. finely chopped green onion
½ c. diced green bell pepper
1½ c. diced celery
2 c. frozen peas
⅓ c. Soy Vinaigrette (page 41)
Whole iceberg or romaine lettuce leaves,
 if desired

Make a day ahead. Recipe doubles easily.

1. In small bowl, cover frozen peas with hot water. Let stand 2 minutes. Drain.

2. In medium bowl, combine thawed peas and other salad ingredients.

3. Prepare Soy Vinaigrette, if not on hand.

4. Toss salad with Soy Vinaigrette, cover and refrigerate.

Suggestions
Serve on whole lettuce leaves, with Oat-Bran Blueberry Muffins (page 101).

NUTRITIONAL INFORMATION PER SERVING:	
Serving size: 1¼ c.	
Calories	233
Fat	20%
Carbohydrates	64%
Protein	9 gm
Sodium	157 mg
Calcium	60 mg
Iron	3 mg
Dietary fiber	9 gm
Cholesterol	0 mg

EXCHANGES:	
Starch/Bread	2½
Vegetable	½
Fat	½

B ☐L☐ ☐D☐ A/S ☐T☐

M **Prep Time:** 10 min.*
C **Cook Time:** 20 min.
Servings: 6
☐S☐ **Yield:** 6 c.

CHILLED ORANGE-RICE SALAD
With Or Without Shrimp

*1 c. diced cooked shrimp (optional)
⅔ c. uncooked white long-grain rice
2 c. thinly sliced celery
½ c. thinly sliced water chestnuts
1¼ c. frozen peas
4 walnuts, shelled and broken
1 large orange, peeled and cut into bite-sized
   pieces
*Lemon-Orange Dressing (page 44)

Salad can be made ahead and refrigerated overnight
in a covered container. Mix well before serving.

   1. Cook rice according to package directions. Drain
and turn into medium bowl. Add shrimp, if desired.
   2. In small bowl, cover frozen peas with hot water.
Let stand 2 minutes. Drain.
   3. Slice water chestnuts and celery. Add to rice mixture, along with peas, orange pieces and walnuts.
   4. Prepare Lemon-Orange Dressing if not on hand.
Pour over salad and serve immediately or chill.

Suggesions
If a creamy dressing is desired, substitute 7 tb. Yogurt-
Poppyseed Dressing (page 43). Nutritional information
will vary. Serve with vegetable sticks, Oat-Bran Muffins,
or Banana Bread.

**NUTRITIONAL
INFORMATION
PER SERVING:**

Salad With Shrimp

Serving size: 1 c.

Calories	178
Fat	8%
Carbohydrates	71%
Protein	9 gm
Sodium	173 mg
Calcium	58 mg
Iron	2 mg
Dietary fiber	2 gm
Cholesterol	41 mg

EXCHANGES:

Starch/Bread	1½
Poultry/Fish/Meat	½
Vegetable	½
Fat	⅓

Salad Without Shrimp

Serving size: 1 c.

Calories	152
Fat	8%
Carbohydrates	81%
Protein	4 gm
Sodium	134 mg
Calcium	41 mg
Iron	2 mg
Dietary fiber	2 gm
Cholesterol	0 mg

EXCHANGES:

Starch/Bread	1½
Vegetable	½
Fat	⅓

| B | L | D | A/S | T |

M   **Prep Time:** 15 min.
     Cook Time: none
C   **Servings:** 8
S   **Yield:** 8 c.

DELIGHTFUL FRUIT SALAD

3 c. diced, unpeeled apples
3 c. diced Bosc pears, unpeeled
2 c. diced, peeled navel oranges
½ c. fresh or frozen unsweetened raspberries
Fruit Dressing (page 46)

Can be made ahead and chilled until ready to serve. Other fruits may be substituted; nutritional information will vary slightly.

1. Combine fruit in refrigerator bowl.
2. In small container, blend dressing ingredients with fork. Pour over fruit, toss to coat. Cover bowl and refrigerate, or serve salad immediately.

Suggestions
This salad can accompany many main dishes or can be served with rolls and milk for breakfast or lunch.

NUTRITIONAL INFORMATION PER SERVING:

Serving size: 1 c.

Calories	109
Fat	6%
Carbohydrates	89%
Protein	1 gm
Sodium	8 mg
Calcium	39 mg
Iron	0 mg
Dietary fiber	4 gm
Cholesterol	0 mg

EXCHANGES:

Fruit	1½
Fat	Tr

M
C

Prep Time: 15 min.
Cook Time: 2 min.
(then chill)

S
Servings: 8
Yield: 5⅓ c.

STRAWBERRY-BANANA SALAD

1 20-oz. bag frozen unsweetened strawberries,
defrosted
1 c. pureed ripe bananas
8 oz. nonfat yogurt
½ c. water
3 pkgs. unflavored gelatin
6 tb. strawberry or raspberry conserve
6 seedless green grapes, sliced, if desired

1. Puree bananas in food processor and measure desired amount. Label and freeze extra to use in another recipe.

2. Puree strawberries in food processor. Add 1 c. pureed banana and blend together until smooth.

3. In small saucepot, sprinkle gelatin over water. Heat, stirring constantly, until gelatin is dissolved.

4. Pour gelatin mixture into feed tube of food processor while processor is running and process until completely blended. Add yogurt and conserve, blending until mixture is smooth.

5. Spray *6-c. gelatin mold* with nonstick coating and pour in mixture. Refrigerate until firm. Unmold and garnish with grapes, if desired.

Suggestions
Serve with a muffin or whole-grain bread for breakfast or as a side dish.

NUTRITIONAL INFORMATION PER SERVING:

Serving size: ⅔ c.

Calories	95
Fat	2%
Carbohydrates	76%
Protein	4 gm
Sodium	26 mg
Calcium	68 mg
Iron	1 mg
Dietary fiber	2 gm
Cholesterol	0 mg

EXCHANGES:

Fruit	1
Milk	⅛

B ☐L☐ ☐D☐ A/S ☐T☐

M
C
☐S☐ **Prep Time:** 10 min.
Cook Time: 3 min.
(then chill)
Servings: 6
Yield: 4½ c.

PEAR-GELATIN SALAD

16-oz. can pears in unsweetened fruit juice
2 pkgs. unflavored gelatin
2½ c. orange juice
Orange slices, if desired

Recipe can be doubled; use a *10-c. mold or bowl.*

1. Drain pears, reserving juice. In *2-qt. sauce pot,* combine orange and pear juice.
2. Puree pears in food processor until smooth.
3. Sprinkle gelatin over juices and mix. Heat mixture, stirring constantly, until gelatin dissolves.
4. Remove from heat. Blend in pureed pears.
5. Spray *5-c. gelatin mold* with nonstick coating and pour in mixture. Cover and refrigerate until firm. Unmold and garnish with orange slices, if desired.

Suggestions
Serve with nonfat yogurt and muffins for lunch, or as a dessert.

NUTRITIONAL INFORMATION PER SERVING:

Serving size: ¾ c.

Calories	78
Fat	3%
Carbohydrates	83%
Protein	3 gm
Sodium	5 mg
Calcium	14 mg
Iron	0 mg
Dietary fiber	2 gm
Cholesterol	0 mg

EXCHANGES:

Fruit	1⅓

B ☐L☐ ☐D☐ A/S ☐T☐

M
C
S **Prep Time:** 5 min.
Cook Time: none
Servings: 4
Yield: ⅓ c.

SOY VINAIGRETTE

1 tsp. honey
   OR ¼ tsp. powdered artificial sweetener
1 tsp. low-sodium soy sauce
1 tb. wine vinegar
2 tb. water
4 tsp. vegetable oil

Recipe can easily be doubled and refrigerated.

1. Combine all ingredients in small, tightly covered container and shake hard. Serve or store.

Suggestions
Serve with Overnight Rice & Bean Salad (page 37), or other salads.

NUTRITIONAL INFORMATION PER SERVING:

Serving size: 4 tsp.

Calories	46
Fat	86%
Carbohydrates	14%
Protein	0 gm
Sodium	46 mg
Calcium	0 mg
Iron	0 mg
Dietary fiber	0 gm
Cholesterol	0 mg

EXCHANGES:

Fat	1

B L D A/S T

M **Prep Time:** 5 min.
C **Cook Time:** none
   Servings: 16-24
S **Yield:** 1-1½ c.

VINAIGRETTE
Regular and Light

REGULAR VINAIGRETTE

½ c. vegetable oil
¼ c. wine vinegar
¼ c. water
1 tsp. honey
   OR ¼ tsp. powdered artificial sweetener
2 tsp. Mrs. Dash® lemon-and-herb seasoning

LIGHT VINAIGRETTE

Add ½ c. orange juice

1. Combine all ingredients in a blender or shake well in tightly covered container.
2. Refrigerate in a covered container until ready to use. Shake well before using.

NUTRITIONAL INFORMATION PER SERVING:

Regular Vinaigrette

Serving size: 1 tb.

Calories	64
Fat	94%
Carbohydrates	6%
Protein	0 gm
Sodium	1 mg
Calcium	0 mg
Iron	0 mg
Dietary fiber	0 gm
Cholesterol	0 mg

EXCHANGES:

Fat	1½

Light Vinaigrette

Serving size: 1 tb.

Calories	45
Fat	89%
Carbohydrates	10%
Protein	0 gm
Sodium	0 mg
Calcium	1 mg
Iron	0 mg
Dietary fiber	0 gm
Cholesterol	0 mg

EXCHANGES:

Fruit	Tr
Fat	1

$\boxed{\text{B}}$ $\boxed{\text{L}}$ $\boxed{\text{D}}$ A/S $\boxed{\text{T}}$

M **Prep Time:** 5 min.
  Cook Time: none
C **Servings:** 6
S **Yield:** ¾ c.

YOGURT-POPPYSEED DRESSING

½ c. nonfat yogurt
1 tb. orange conserve
2 tb. grated orange rind
2 tb. reduced-calorie and -fat sour cream
½ tsp. poppy seeds

Recipe can be easily doubled.

1. Combine all ingredients in small container and blend well with fork. Serve or store. Mix before serving.

Suggestions
Use on lettuce or fruit salads.

NUTRITIONAL INFORMATION PER SERVING:

Serving size: 2 tb.

Calories	26
Fat	20%
Carbohydrates	53%
Protein	1 gm
Sodium	21 mg
Calcium	41 mg
Iron	0 mg
Dietary fiber	0 gm
Cholesterol	0 mg

EXCHANGES:

Fruit	Tr
Milk	⅓
Fat	Tr

B $\boxed{\text{L}}$ $\boxed{\text{D}}$ A/S $\boxed{\text{T}}$

M **Prep Time:** 5 min.
  Cook Time: none
C **Servings:** 5
S **Yield:** ⅔ c.

YOGURT-DIJON DRESSING

½ c. nonfat yogurt
1 tsp. Dijon-style mustard
1 tb. orange conserve
1 tb. reduced-calorie and -fat mayonnaise
½ tsp. celery seeds

Recipe doubles easily.

1. Combine all ingredients in small container, blend with fork. Serve or store. Mix well before serving.

Suggestions
Toss with salad greens combined with fruit slices.

NUTRITIONAL INFORMATION PER SERVING:

Serving size: 2 tb.

Calories	31
Fat	33%
Carbohydrates	45%
Protein	1 gm
Sodium	31 mg
Calcium	50 mg
Iron	0 mg
Dietary fiber	0 gm
Cholesterol	1 mg

EXCHANGES:

Fruit	Tr
Milk	⅕
Fat	⅕

B ☐L☐ ☐D☐ A/S ☐T☐

M **Prep Time:** 5 min.
  Cook Time: none
C **Servings:** 2
S **Yield:** ½ c.

ORANGE-YOGURT DRESSING

⅓ c. orange juice
3 tb. nonfat yogurt
¼ tsp. fresly ground pepper

Recipe can be easily doubled. Store in refrigerator.

1. In small container, blend together yogurt and orange juice. Add pepper. When preparing larger quantities, combine ingredients in blender.

Suggestion
Toss salad greens with dressing.

NUTRITIONAL INFORMATION PER SERVING:

Serving size: ¼ c.

Calories	29
Fat	4%
Carbohydrates	76%
Protein	2 gm
Sodium	17 mg
Calcium	48 mg
Iron	0 mg
Dietary fiber	0 gm
Cholesterol	0 mg

EXCHANGES:

Fruit	½
Milk	Tr

☐B☐ ☐L☐ ☐D☐ A/S ☐T☐

M **Prep Time:** 5 min.
  Cook Time: none
C **Servings:** 6
S **Yield:** ½ c.

LEMON-ORANGE DRESSING

2 tsp. low-sodium soy sauce
1 tb. orange conserve
1 tb. lemon juice
5 tb. orange juice

Recipe doubles easily and can be stored in refrigerator.

1. Combine all ingredients in small container.
Cover tightly and shake well.

Suggestions
Serve with Rice and Orange Salad (page 38) or on cold rice or fruit salads (omit soy sauce for fruit salads).

NUTRITIONAL INFORMATION PER SERVING:

Serving size: 4 tsp.

Calories	13
Fat	2%
Carbohydrates	93%
Protein	0 gm
Sodium	61 mg
Calcium	2 mg
Iron	0 mg
Dietary fiber	0 gm
Cholesterol	0 mg

EXCHANGES:

Fruit	⅕

B L D A/S T

CHICKEN OR FISH MARINADE

1 tsp. honey
  OR ¼ tsp. powdered artificial sweetener
2 tsp. low-sodium soy sauce
2 tb. wine vinegar
1 tb. lemon juice
1 tb. vegetable oil
3 tb. water

Recipe doubles easily. Store in refrigerator.

1. Combine all ingredients in a small container.
Cover tightly and shake well. Serve or store.

Suggesions
Used as a marinade for a stir fry dish or as dressing on
an overnight salad.

**NUTRITIONAL
INFORMATION
PER SERVING:**

Serving size: 1 tb.

Calories	19
Fat	78%
Carbohydrates	22%
Protein	0 gm
Sodium	46 mg
Calcium	0 mg
Iron	0 mg
Dietary fiber	0 gm
Cholesterol	0 mg

EXCHANGES:

Fat	⅓

B L D A/S T

VEGETABLE MARINADE

4 tsp. orange or pineapple conserve
1 tb. low-sodium soy sauce
2 tb. wine vinegar
1 tb. lemon juice
2 tsp. vegetable oil
2 tb. water

1. Combine ingredients in a small container.
Cover tightly and shake well. Serve or store.

Suggestions
A delicious marinade for any cold vegetables.

**NUTRITIONAL
INFORMATION
PER SERVING:**

Serving size: 1 tb.

Calories	30
Fat	84%
Carbohydrates	16%
Protein	0 gm
Sodium	68 mg
Calcium	0 mg
Iron	0 mg
Dietary fiber	0 gm
Cholesterol	0 mg

EXCHANGES:

Fruit	Tr
Fat	1

B L D A/S T

M   **Prep Time:** 5 min.
    Cook Time: none
C   **Servings:** 6
S   **Yield:** 6 tb.

FRUIT DRESSING

2 tb. reduced-calorie and -fat sour cream
2 tb. nonfat yogurt
1 tb. raspberry conserve
1 tb. frozen orange juice concentrate

Recipe easily doubles. Store in refrigerator.

1. Combine ingredients in small container and blend well with fork. Serve or store.

Suggestions
Serve with Delightful Fruit Salad (page 39) or on any fruit salad.

NUTRITIONAL INFORMATION PER SERVING:

Serving size: 1 tb.

Calories	20
Fat	19%
Carbohydrates	64%
Protein	1 gm
Sodium	10 mg
Calcium	10 mg
Iron	0 mg
Dietary fiber	0 gm
Cholesterol	0 mg

EXCHANGES:

Fruit	⅕
Milk	Tr

46 *Menu for Life*

VEGETABLES

Clockwise from bottom: Twice-Baked Potatoes (page 62), All-Around Potato,
Marinated Vegetables.

INDEX

Great Boiled Potatoes   50
All-Around Potato   51
Herbed Potato Sticks   52
Sweet Potatoes   53
Sweet Potatoes or Carrots With Sauce   54
Fancy Steamed Vegetables   55
Marinated Vegetables   56

I f you thought you had to forego potatoes to keep your scales under control, think again. All-Around Potatoes just might change your mind. Not only are they low in calories, they're low in fat.

So are all the vegetable recipes in this chapter—from Marinated Vegetables to Sweet Potatoes With Sauce.

For a fast-food treat your family will love, try Herbed Potato Sticks. They'll make you forget all about french fries—and they're a snap to make.

Hints

- Steam vegetables in a stovetop steamer, which is inexpensive and fits inside most pots. Or prepare in a microwave oven, following manufacturer's instructions. Do not overcook.
- White and sweet potatoes can be boiled in the skin or cooked in a microwave oven, cooled, wrapped and refrigerated. They will keep for several days. Prepare recipe when convenient.

Equivalents

8 c. raw diced vegetables = approximately 6 c. cooked vegetables.

M   **Prep Time:** 10 min.
     Cook Time: 20 min.
C   **Servings:** 6
S   **Yield:** 4 c.

GREAT BOILED POTATOES

Lemon And Herb, Orange-Basil Or Spicy

1½ lbs. scrubbed potatoes
1 medium onion, peeled and quartered
1 tb. vegetable oil
Freshly ground pepper

LEMON AND HERB POTATOES

1 tb. lemon juice
1½ tsp. parsley
1½ tsp. Mrs. Dash® lemon-and-herb seasoning
Lemon wedges, if desired

ORANGE-BASIL POTATOES

2 tb. orange juice
1½ tsp. basil
1 tsp. Mrs. Dash® original blend seasoning

SPICY POTATOES

1 medium tomato, diced
1½ tsp. Mrs. Dash® extra-spicy seasoning

Recipe can be made ahead and reheated in microwave oven.

1. Scrub potatoes and cut them in eighths. Combine with onions in *4-qt. stock pot.* Cover with water and bring to a boil. Cook partially covered for 15 to 20 minutes or until potatoes are soft but not overcooked.
2. Meanwhile, in small bowl, combine remaining ingredients (except lemon wedges).
3. Drain cooked potatoes and onions in colander. In same pot, heat remaining ingredients. Stir in potatoes and onions, tossing to coat. Serve immediately or store. Garnish Lemon and Herb Potatoes with lemon wedges for extra zest.

Suggestions
Serve as a side dish or top with 1 tb. parmesan cheese or 1 oz. mozzarella cheese and serve as a main dish.

NUTRITIONAL INFORMATION PER SERVING:

Any version

Serving size: ⅔ c.

Calories	158
Fat	14%
Carbohydrates	78%
Protein	3 gm
Sodium	11 mg
Calcium	20 mg
Iron	2 mg
Dietary fiber	3 gm
Cholesterol	0 mg

EXCHANGES:

Starch/Bread	1½
Vegetable	½
Fat	½

B L D A/S T

Prep Time: 3 min.*
Cook Time: 3-5 min.
Servings: 1

ALL-AROUND POTATO
With Parmesan Or Mozzarella Cheese

*1 medium potato, scrubbed and boiled
1 tb. low-fat mayonnaise
1 tb. skim milk
½ tsp. basil
¼ tsp. freshly ground pepper, if desired
1 oz. part-skim mozzarella cheese, grated or
    thinly sliced
    OR 1 tb. grated parmesan cheese

Recipe can be made ahead and refrigerated. Boil
several potatoes at once and refrigerate until needed.

  1. Slice potato and arrange pieces on oven-safe
plate or in baking dish so that they overlap slightly.
  2. In small bowl, mix mayonnaise, milk and spices
with a fork.
  3. Drizzle mayonnaise mixture over potato slices.
  4. Top with mozzarella or parmesan cheese. If
preparing ahead, refrigerate.
  5. Bake at 350 degrees for 3 to 5 minutes in oven or
toaster oven, or in microwave oven on medium-high for
3 minutes. Bake until heated thoroughly and cheese is
bubbly. Increase baking time if dish has been refrigerated. Serve immediately.

Suggestions
Top potatoes with steamed vegetables before adding
cheese. Prepare in a casserole as a side dish by layer-
ing potatoes, vegetables, sauce and cheese.

**NUTRITIONAL
INFORMATION
PER SERVING:**

**With Mozzarella
Cheese**

Serving size: 1 potato

Calories	307
Fat	26%
Carbohydrates	60%
Protein	12 gm
Sodium	155 mg
Calcium	238 mg
Iron	3 mg
Dietary fiber	4 gm
Cholesterol	21 mg

EXCHANGES:

Starch/Bread	2
Poultry/Fish/Meat	1
Fat	1½

With Parmesan Cheese

Serving size: 1 potato

Calories	299
Fat	25%
Carbohydrates	61%
Protein	10 gm
Sodium	286 mg
Calcium	248 mg
Iron	3 mg
Dietary fiber	4 gm
Cholesterol	16 mg

EXCHANGES:

Starch/Bread	2
Poultry/Fish/Meat	1
Fat	1½

HERBED POTATO STICKS

3-4 large potatoes (2 lbs.)
5 tb. water
2 tb. vegetable oil
1½ tsp. paprika
2 tb. Mrs. Dash® lemon-and-herb seasoning

Steps 1 through 4 can be done ahead. Cover
and refrigerate until ready to bake. Recipe does not
reheat well.

   1. In a *1-c. measuring cup* mix oil, water and spices
with a fork until well blended.
   2. Scrub potatoes and slice lengthwise to resemble
chunky french fries. In a large bowl, pour spice mixture
over potatoes and toss to coat completely.
   3. Spray *two 10″ x 15″ baking sheets* with nonstick
coating. Preheat oven to 400 degrees.
   4. Using a fork, place potato sticks on baking sheets.
Drizzle remaining spice mixture over them.
   5. Bake for 30 minutes or until the thickest pieces
are done. Serve immediately.

**NUTRITIONAL
INFORMATION
PER SERVING:**

Serving size: ⅙ of recipe

Calories	198
Fat	21%
Carbohydrates	72%
Protein	4 gm
Sodium	16 mg
Calcium	14 mg
Iron	2 mg
Dietary fiber	3 gm
Cholesterol	0 mg

EXCHANGES:

Starch/Bread	1½
Fat	1

| B | L | D | A/S | T |

SWEET POTATOES
With Parsley Or Cheese

2 sweet potatoes (1 lb.)
1 tb. vegetable oil
**   OR 2 oz. grated mozzarella cheese**
1 tsp. parsley

Can be made ahead and refrigerated.

1. In *3-qt. stock pot,* cover sweet potatoes with water and cook over medium heat, partially covered, until soft (about 30 minutes). Drain and let stand 5 minutes. Peel potatoes; skin should come off easily.

2. Spray a *shallow baking dish* with nonstick coating. Slice sweet potatoes in half and arrange in dish. Brush with oil or top with grated cheese. Sprinkle with parsley. Wrap and refrigerate or heat in microwave on medium high 2 to 4 minutes. or conventional oven at 350 degrees for 10 minutes or until heated thoroughly.

Suggestions
Assemble the night before and serve Sweet Potatoes With Cheese as a quick breakfast. Sweet Potatoes With Parsley is a good choice with poultry, fish or meat entrees.

NUTRITIONAL INFORMATION PER SERVING:

With Parsley

Serving size: ½ potato

Calories	148
Fat	21%
Carbohydrates	74%
Protein	2 gm
Sodium	12 mg
Calcium	33 mg
Iron	1 mg
Dietary fiber	3 gm
Cholesterol	0 mg

EXCHANGES:

Starch/Bread	1½
Fat	½

With Cheese

Serving size: ½ potato

Calories	154
Fat	14%
Carbohydrates	72%
Protein	5 gm
Sodium	79 mg
Calcium	126 mg
Iron	1 mg
Dietary fiber	3 gm
Cholesterol	8 mg

EXCHANGES:

Starch/Bread	1½
Poultry/Fish/Meat	¼
Fat	¼

SWEET POTATOES OR CARROTS WITH SAUCE

2 sweet potatoes (1 lb.)
   OR 1½ lbs. carrots
¾ c. thinly sliced onion
¾ c. orange juice
1 tb. low-sodium soy sauce
1 tb. cornstarch
½ c. thinly sliced water chestnuts
2 tb. water

Recipe can be made ahead and reheated.

   1. Scrub sweet potatoes. In *3-qt. saucepot,* cover with water and bring to a boil. Cook partially covered for 30 minutes or until soft. Drain, let stand 5 minutes and peel. For carrots, slice and steam until tender.

   2. Meanwhile, prepare sauce. Spray *1-qt. saucepot* with nonstick coating. In 2 tb. water, cook onions, covered, until soft (about 3 to 5 minutes).

   3. In measuring cup, mix together orange juice, soy sauce and cornstarch. Pour over softened onions and cook, stirring constantly, until thick and bubbly. Blend in water chestnuts.

   4. Arrange potatoes or carrots in serving dish. Drizzle with sauce. Serve immediately or cover and refrigerate. Reheat in microwave or conventional oven until heated thoroughly.

Suggestions
Serve with fish or poultry.

NUTRITIONAL INFORMATION PER SERVING:

Sweet Potatoes
Serving size: ½ potato with sauce

Calories	173
Fat	2%
Carbohydrates	92%
Protein	3 gm
Sodium	152 mg
Calcium	47 mg
Iron	1 mg
Dietary fiber	3 gm
Cholesterol	0 mg

EXCHANGES:

Starch/Bread	1½
Vegetable	½
Fruit	Tr

Carrots
Serving size: 1½ c. with sauce

Calories	104
Fat	3%
Carbohydrates	89%
Protein	2 gm
Sodium	179 mg
Calcium	45 mg
Iron	1 mg
Dietary fiber	4 gm
Cholesterol	0 mg

EXCHANGES:

Starch/Bread	Tr
Vegetable	2½
Fruit	Tr

B L D A/S T

M
C
S

Prep Time: 10 min.
Cook Time: 5-10 min.
Servings: 6

FANCY STEAMED VEGETABLES

1½ lb. fresh asparagus, washed and trimmed
    (20-24 spears)
½ large onion, sliced thin
¼ red bell pepper, sliced thin

Recipe can be made ahead and reheated. Use any
vegetables desired.

1. Steam together asparagus, onion and bell
pepper until asparagus and onion are tender. Arrange
in serving dish, placing bell pepper slices on top. Serve
or store.

Suggestions
Serve with any main dish.

**NUTRITIONAL
INFORMATION
PER SERVING:**

Serving size: 3-4 spears

Calories	33
Fat	9%
Carbohydrates	61%
Protein	3 gm
Sodium	5 mg
Calcium	31 mg
Iron	1 mg
Dietary fiber	2 gm
Cholesterol	0 mg

EXCHANGES:

Vegetable	1

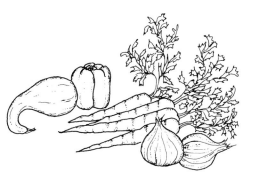

B L D A/S T

MARINATED VEGETABLES

2 c. thinly sliced raw or steamed carrots
2 c. chopped, peeled yellow crookneck squash
2 c. chopped zucchini
½ c. diced red bell pepper
1 c. thinly sliced onion
4 tsp. orange or pineapple conserve
1 tb. low-sodium soy sauce
2 tb. wine vinegar
1 tb. lemon juice
2 tsp. vegetable oil
2 tb. water

For best results, marinate overnight.

1. In storage container, combine vegetables.
2. Mix marinade ingredients and pour over vegetables.
3. Cover and refrigerate. Stir several times while vegetables are marinating.

Suggestions
Serve with poultry, fish or meat or with All-Around Potato (page 51).

**NUTRITIONAL
INFORMATION
PER SERVING:**

Serving size: ¾ c.

Calories	36
Fat	27%
Carbohydrates	62%
Protein	1 gm
Sodium	62 mg
Calcium	17 mg
Iron	0 mg
Dietary fiber	2 gm
Cholesterol	0 mg

EXCHANGES:

Vegetable	1
Fat	⅕

MEATLESS Meals

Clockwise from left: Stuffed Pasta Shells, Basic Tomato Sauce (page 22), Hearty Casserole (with cheese), Surprise Quiche (center, on cutting board), Cornmeal-Bean Squares (top and bottom, on cutting board).

INDEX

Hearty Casserole   60
Meatless Shepherd's Pie   61
Twice-Baked Potatoes   62
Surprise Quiche   63
Tofu Lasagna   64
Stuffed Pasta Shells   65
Simple Pasta-Vegetable Plate   66
Basic Rice   67
Simple Rice and Bean Casserole   68
Cornmeal-Bean Squares   69
Healthy Burritos   70
Pita Pockets   71
Undeviled Eggs   72

Going meatless doesn't necessarily mean going without. There's something right for every meal of the day among the following recipes.

Many of the recipes in this section were created to ensure protein complementation—the process of selecting certain foods to combine nine essential amino acids in a meal. The key ingredients in this matching process are grains, legumes, seeds and nuts—all of which are easy to prepare. Keep an open mind!

Equivalents

1 c. dry rice = approximately 3 c. cooked

1 c. dried legumes = approximately 2½ c. cooked

Preparation of Legumes

1. Rinse dried beans in a strainer, discarding any damaged beans or pebbles.

2. In a pot large enough to accommodate cooked beans (they triple in volume during soaking), cover beans with water and bring to a boil. Cook, stirring continuously, for 2 minutes.

3. Remove from heat. Let soak 1 to 2 hours.

4. Drain and rinse. Cover with water and cook partially covered for 45-60 minutes or until beans are tender but not mushy.

Hints

• Reduce meal preparation time by cooking beans or rice in volume and freezing in premeasured amounts for later use. Store in labeled, self-sealing freezer bags.

Defrost and reheat in microwave oven or by covering bag with warm water.

• Canned beans may be substituted for dried beans in any recipe. Nutritional information will vary slightly.

Tofu: The Great Pretender

Made from soybeans, tofu looks almost like a soft-curd cheese. It has virtually no taste of its own—which, oddly enough, is one of its greatest assets, for tofu can take on the taste, texture and appearance of many foods ... from meat to ice cream. Versatile and cholesterol-free, tofu combines well with grains, seeds or nuts to make a complete protein.

Tofu comes in both regular curd and firm curd; the nutritional information for these recipes is based on regular-curd tofu.

Hints

• Purchase only tofu that has been refrigerated; be sure to check the expiration date.

• Cover tofu with fresh water and store it in the refrigerator in an air-tight container. Change the water every few days.

• To use, rinse, pat dry with paper towels and follow recipe.

See also, Protein Complementation, page 4.

B L D A/S T

Prep Time: 15 min.*
Cook Time: 7-15 min.
Servings: 6
Yield: 9 c.

M
C
S

HEARTY CASSEROLE
Cheese or Tomato

HEARTY CHEESE CASSEROLE

*2 c. cooked kidney beans or favorite beans
　(if frozen, partially defrost)
*2 c. cooked brown rice
　(if frozen, partially defrost)
3 c. carrots, diced
3 c. red, yellow or green bell peppers
　(or combination), diced
2 c. leeks, thinly sliced
4 oz. mozzarella cheese, grated
⅓ c. reduced-fat and -calorie mayonnaise
2 tsp. lemon juice
1 tsp. Mrs. Dash® lemon-and-herb seasoning
½ tsp. freshly ground pepper
Lemon wedges

HEARTY TOMATO CASSEROLE

*2 c. cooked kidney beans or favorite beans
　(if frozen, partially defrost)
*2 c. cooked brown rice
　(if frozen, partially defrost)
*2 c. Basic Tomato Sauce (page 22)
8 c. diced vegetables listed above
2 tb. vegetable oil
2 tsp. Mrs. Dash® original blend seasoning

Recipe can be made ahead and refrigerated until
needed. Cheese casserole does not freeze well but
tomato casserole does.

1. Steam vegetables until tender.
2. In large bowl, gently combine all ingredients.
3. Spray 2½-qt. *casserole* with nonstick coating.
Turn in combined ingredients.
4. In oven preheated to 350 degrees, bake covered
for 15 minutes. Or bake covered in microwave oven for
6-7 minutes on medium-high and for 1 minute on high.
Increase baking time if recipe was refrigerated before
cooking or if rice or beans are partially frozen. Serve.

Suggestions
Garnish cheese casserole with lemon wedges. Serve
either casserole with a gelatin salad and warm bread.

**NUTRITIONAL
INFORMATION
PER SERVING:**

Hearty Cheese Casserole

Serving size: 1½ c.

Calories	282
Fat	24%
Carbohydrates	59%
Protein	12 gm
Sodium	148 mg
Calcium	188 mg
Iron	3 mg
Dietary fiber	11 gm
Cholesterol	15 mg

EXCHANGES:

Starch/Bread	2
Poultry/Fish/Meat	½
Vegetable	1½
Fat	1⅓

Hearty Tomato Casserole

Serving size: 1½ c.

Calories	275
Fat	18%
Carbohydrates	69%
Protein	9 gm
Sodium	68 mg
Calcium	74 mg
Iron	4 mg
Dietary fiber	11 gm
Cholesterol	0 mg

EXCHANGES:

Starch/Bread	2
Vegetable	2½
Fat	1

B L D A/S T

MEATLESS SHEPHERD'S PIE
See Also Lean Shepherd's Pie With Meat
(page 92)

Filling
*1⅓ c. cooked kidney beans, lightly mashed
2 tb. vegetable oil
1 oz. mozzarella cheese, diced
1 15-oz. can unsalted tomato sauce
1 garlic clove, chopped
1 tsp. each basil and oregano
½ tsp. pepper
1 c. chopped onion
2 c. diced carrots, fresh or frozen
2 c. diced broccoli, fresh or frozen
2 c. diced cauliflower, fresh or frozen

Topping
10 c. peeled and diced potatoes
      (approx. 3¾ lbs.)
1 whole medium onion, skinned
2 tsp. oregano
½ tsp. pepper
½ c. ½%-fat cottage cheese
2 tb. grated parmesan cheese
2 tb. ½%-fat buttermilk (more, if necessary)
1 medium tomato, sliced, if desired

NUTRITIONAL INFORMATION PER SERVING:

Serving size:
⅛ of 9″ x 13″ pan or
¼ of 9″ round pan

Calories	332
Fat	14%
Carbohydrates	73%
Protein	12 gm
Sodium	92 mg
Calcium	121 mg
Iron	2 mg
Dietary fiber	7 gm
Cholesterol	4 mg

EXCHANGES:

Starch/Bread	3
Poultry/Fish/Meat	¼
Vegetable	2
Fat	1

Recipe freezes well. Can be made ahead in two 9″ round pans (4 servings each). Eat one, freeze one. Heat in conventional oven. Microwave changes potato consistency.

1. Steam filling vegetables until tender. In large bowl, blend together mozzarella cheese, tomato sauce, beans, oil, garlic and spices. Stir in vegetables. Spray baking dish with nonstick coating. Turn in to *one 9″ x 13″ or two 9″ round baking dishes.*

2. Meanwhile, combine diced potatoes and whole onion in *6-qt. stock pot.* Cover with water and bring to a boil. Cook partially covered until potatoes are soft enough to mash (about 20 minutes).

3. While potatoes are cooking, puree cottage cheese in food processor for 3-4 minutes, scraping sides occasionally, until it is the consistency of sour cream.

4. Drain cooked potatoes in colander, discarding onion, and return to pot. Add buttermilk and mash with hand masher or electric mixer. Do not overbeat. Stir in spices, cottage cheese and parmesan cheese.

5. Top filling with potato mixture and smooth to edges with a spatula. Garnish with tomato slices.

6. In oven preheated to 350 degrees, bake 15 minutes or until thoroughly heated and top is slightly browned. Serve. Or freeze unbaked.

Suggestions
Serve with a large tossed salad and bread sticks.

TWICE-BAKED POTATOES

See Also Twice-Baked Potato With
Chicken (page 87)

4 medium baking potatoes (1½ lbs.)
1 c. diced carrots, fresh or frozen unsalted
1 c. diced broccoli, fresh or frozen unsalted
1 c. diced onion
4 tsp. vegetable oil
2 tb. grated parmesan cheese
Freshly ground pepper to taste
4 tb. Healthy Topping (page 26)
Bell pepper slices, pimento strips or tomato
roses, if desired

Prepare ahead in any quantity. Cover and refrigerate
or wrap individually and freeze. To serve, defrost and
heat through.

1. Bake potatoes at 400 degrees for 45 to 50
minutes. (To speed baking, prebake in microwave oven
but bake the last 15 minutes in conventional oven to
crisp potato skins.)
2. While potatoes are baking, dice and steam
vegetables and onion until they are tender. Set aside.
3. Prepare Healthy Topping, if not already prepared.
4. Remove potatoes from oven and let cool for 5
minutes for easier handling. Holding potato with pot-
holder, slice lengthwise to remove top quarter. With
small spoon, gently scoop pulp from top and bottom
skins, being careful not to break them. Reserve skins.
With a fork, lightly mash potato pulp. Mix in oil, cheese
and pepper, then vegetables.
5. Stuff potato mixture back into skins. They will be
very full. Put potato tops in place or garnish with bell
pepper slices, pimento strips or tomato roses. Return
to oven and heat thoroughly, or cover and refrigerate
or freeze.

Suggestions
Makes a meal in itself. Serve with fresh fruit or a gelatin
mold and tossed salad. Or remove from freezer in the
morning and reheat in microwave oven at work for
lunch.

NUTRITIONAL
INFORMATION
PER SERVING:

Serving size: 1 stuffed
potato

Calories	289
Fat	18%
Carbohydrates	68%
Protein	10 gm
Sodium	95 mg
Calcium	99 mg
Iron	3 mg
Dietary fiber	6 gm
Cholesterol	4 mg

EXCHANGES:

Starch/Bread	2
Poultry/Fish/Meat	½
Vegetable	1½
Fat	1⅓

Prep Time: 20 min.
Cook Time: 50 min.
Servings: 12
Yield: (1) 9″ x 13″ pan

SURPRISE QUICHE

2 10-oz. packages of frozen spinach, defrosted,
    drained and squeezed dry
3 egg whites, beaten with a fork
1 c. ½%-fat cottage cheese
2 oz. canned whole green chilies, drained,
    seeded, and finely chopped
2-oz. jar chopped pimento, drained
4-oz. can mushroom pieces, drained and
    finely chopped
1 clove garlic, finely chopped
¾ c. green onion, chopped
2 tsp. Mrs. Dash® lemon-and-herb seasoning
½ tsp. pepper
8 oz. part-skim mozzarella cheese
1 lb. regular curd tofu
3 tb. unbleached all-purpose flour

Recipe can be doubled, prepared ahead and
refrigerated to be baked later. Bake in conventional
oven. May be reheated in microwave oven.
Freezes well.

1. In large bowl, blend spinach, egg whites, cottage
cheese, chilies, pimento, mushrooms, garlic, onions,
lemon-and-herb seasoning and pepper.
2. Grate mozzarella cheese and tofu in food
processor.
3. Blend tofu-cheese mixture into spinach mixture.
Sprinkle with flour and blend again. Preheat oven to
350 degrees.
4. Spray *9″x13″ baking dish* with nonstick coating.
Spread the ingredients evenly. Bake uncovered for
50 minutes.
5. Remove from oven and let stand for 10 minutes.
Cut and serve immediately or store for later use.

Suggestions
Serve with whole-grain rolls, carrot sticks and a fresh
fruit salad with Yogurt-Poppyseed Dressing (page 43).
Cut into 24-36 pieces and serve as an appetizer.

**NUTRITIONAL
INFORMATION
PER SERVING:**

Serving size:
3″ x 3¼″ piece

Calories	119
Fat	35%
Carbohydrates	24%
Protein	13 gm
Sodium	148 mg
Calcium	252 mg
Iron	2 mg
Dietary fiber	1 gm
Cholesterol	12 mg

EXCHANGES:

Poultry/Fish/Meat	1⅓
Vegetable	½
Fat	1

M   **Prep Time:** 20 min.*
C   **Cook Time:** 25 min.
    Servings: 4
S   **Yield:** (1) 8" x 8" pan

TOFU LASAGNA

See Also Lasagna With Meat Sauce
(page 93)

*2½ c. **Basic Tomato Sauce (page 22), warmed**
 3 c. **diced red and green bell peppers**
 1 c. **chopped onion**
 4 oz. **part-skim mozzarella cheese, grated**
 8 oz. **regular curd tofu, broken into small pieces**
 4-oz. **can mushrooms, drained**
 ½-lb. **package lasagna noodles**
 Grated parmesan cheese, if desired

Recipe can be doubled and assembled in a 9" x 13"
baking pan. Freezes well.

1. Cook lasagna noodles according to package
directions.
2. Meanwhile, steam green peppers and onions.
3. Preheat oven to 350 degrees. Spray *8"x8"*
baking pan with nonstick coating.
4. Spread ½ c. sauce on bottom of pan. Layer
lasagna noodles, mushrooms, peppers, onions,
mozzarella cheese and tofu. Cover with 1 c. tomato
sauce. Repeat.
5. Bake uncovered for 25 minutes. Remove from
oven and let stand for 10 minutes. Cut and serve.

Suggestions
Top Tofu Lasagna square with additional tomato sauce,
if desired. Serve with warm bread or rolls and a large
tossed salad.

NUTRITIONAL INFORMATION PER SERVING:	
Serving size: 4" x 4" square	
Calories	282
Fat	25%
Carbohydrates	51%
Protein	18 gm
Sodium	157 mg
Calcium	297 mg
Iron	5 mg
Dietary fiber	3 gm
Cholesterol	16 mg

EXCHANGES:	
Starch/Bread	1
Poultry/Fish/Meat	2
Vegetable	1½
Fat	½

B L D A/S T

M **Prep Time:** 30 min.*
C **Cook Time:** 5-15 min.
   Servings: 6
S **Yield:** 24 shells

STUFFED PASTA SHELLS

NUTRITIONAL INFORMATION PER SERVING:

Serving size: 4 shells with sauce

Calories	246
Fat	35%
Carbohydrates	34%
Protein	19 gm
Sodium	322 mg
Calcium	419 mg
Iron	3 mg
Dietary fiber	1 gm
Cholesterol	26 mg

EXCHANGES:

Starch/Bread	½
Poultry/Fish/Meat	3½
Vegetable	1
Fat	1½

*3⅓ c. Basic Tomato Sauce (page 22)
½ lb. regular curd tofu
½ lb. part-skim mozzarella cheese
⅓ c. grated parmesan cheese
½ c. fresh parsley, chopped
⅓ c. skim milk
½ tsp. pepper
1 tsp. basil
2 egg whites, beaten
Large pasta shells, 5-6 ozs. (approx. 24)

Recipe can be made ahead and frozen or refrigerated until ready for baking. Shells can be reheated after baking.

1. Cook pasta shells according to package directions.

2. Meanwhile, grate mozzarella cheese and tofu in food processor.

3. In large bowl, combine egg whites, tofu, mozzarella cheese, parmesan cheese, parsley, milk, pepper and basil.

4. Heat Basic Tomato Sauce.

5. Begin stuffing shells with tofu-cheese mixture as soon as they are cool enough to handle. A tablespoon works well for stuffing the shells.

6. Spray two *9"x10" round baking dishes* with nonstick coating. Spread a small amount of sauce on pan and arrange stuffed shells. Drizzle shells with remaining sauce so they do not dry out while baking.

7. Lay a piece of foil over pan (do not seal edges) and bake in oven preheated to 350 degrees for 15 minutes or until heated through. Or bake uncovered 4-5 minutes on medium-high in microwave oven. Garnish with parsley, if desired. Serve.

Suggestions
Serve with a large tossed salad, warm bread and sliced fresh fruit. May be served as an appetizer.

B L D A/S T

M **Prep Time:** 10 min.*
C **Cook Time:** 15 min.
   Servings: 1
S **Yield:** 2¼ c.

SIMPLE PASTA VEGETABLE PLATE

*⅓ c. Basic Tomato Sauce (page 22)
1 c. whole-grain pasta
1½ c. green pepper, carrots and onions
1 tb. grated parmesan cheese

Recipe can be doubled or assembled ahead on seving plate.

1. Cook pasta according to package directions.
2. Meanwhile, steam vegetables and heat sauce.
3. Place cooked, drained pasta on plate. Top with vegetables, sauce and cheese. Serve or refrigerate. Reheat in microwave for 1-2 minutes on high.

Suggestions
Serve with Delightful Fruit Salad (page 39) and whole-grain roll.

NUTRITIONAL INFORMATION PER SERVING:

Serving size: 2¼ c.

Calories	295
Fat	10%
Carbohydrates	74%
Protein	12 gm
Sodium	175 mg
Calcium	155 mg
Iron	4 mg
Dietary fiber	6 gm
Cholesterol	5 mg

EXCHANGES:

Starch/Bread	2
Poultry/Meat/Fish	½
Vegetable	3½

B   L   D   A/S   T

M   **Prep Time:** 15 min.
C   **Cook Time:** 30 min.
S   **Servings:** 27
    Yield: 9 c.

BASIC RICE
Brown or White

BROWN RICE
1 tb. vegetable oil
1 c. chopped onion
1 clove garlic, finely chopped
½ red bell pepper, sliced into long thin strips
½ green bell pepper, sliced into long thin strips
3 c. uncooked brown rice
4 c. water

WHITE RICE
Above ingredients (omit brown rice)
3 c. long-grain white rice
Decrease water to 3½ c.

Freezes well or keeps for up to 1 week in a refrigerated air-tight container. Freeze in self-sealing freezer bags in pre-measured portions. Defrost by placing bag in hot water or by defrosting in microwave oven.

1. Spray *4 to 6-qt. stock pot* with nonstick coating. Heat oil on medium. Add onion, garlic and bell peppers. Heat 4 to 6 minutes, stirring often, until ingredients are partially cooked but not browned.
2. Add rice. On medium-high heat, continue cooking and stirring until rice is coated with oil and begins to brown. Rice should turn a honey color.
3. Add water, stir and bring to a boil. Reduce heat to a low boil. Cover and simmer for 30 minutes (20 minutes for white rice) or until water evaporates and rice is tender but firm.
4. When rice is done, remove lid to let steam escape. Cook and stir for 2 minutes longer. Serve, refrigerate or freeze.

Suggestions
To make this dish a complemented protein, add 1 tb. of your favorite seeds and/or nuts. Add ¼ c. cooked wild rice for added color and texture.

NUTRITIONAL INFORMATION PER SERVING:

Brown Rice

Serving size: ⅓ c.

Calories	85
Fat	10%
Carbohydrates	82%
Protein	2 gm
Sodium	0 mg
Calcium	10 mg
Iron	0 mg
Dietary fiber	3 gm
Cholesterol	0 mg

EXCHANGES:

Starch/Bread	1
Fat	Tr

White Rice

Serving size: ⅓ c.

Calories	82
Fat	6%
Carbohydrates	87%
Protein	1 gm
Sodium	2 mg
Calcium	9 mg
Iron	1 mg
Dietary fiber	1 gm
Cholesterol	0 mg

EXCHANGES:

Starch/Bread	1
Fat	Tr

M
C
S

Prep Time: 10 min.*
Cook Time: 5-15 min.
Servings: 8
Yield: 8 c.

SIMPLE RICE & BEAN CASSEROLE

*4 c. Basic Rice (page 67)
*4 c. cooked kidney beans or favorite beans
*1 c. Basic Tomato Sauce (page 22)
  3 oz. part-skim mozzarella cheese, grated

Recipe can be doubled. Need not be baked before freezing.

  1. Preheat oven to 400 degrees. Spray *3-qt. casserole* with nonstick coating.
  2. Toss ingredients in a large bowl until well mixed. Place in casserole.
  3. Cover and bake 15 minutes or until heated through. Or bake partially covered in microwave oven for 3-4 minutes on medium-high and for one minute on high. Serve.

Suggestions
Serve with a large tossed salad with Vinaigrette Light (page 42) and sliced fresh fruit.

**NUTRITIONAL
INFORMATION
PER SERVING:**

Serving size: 1 c.

Calories	270
Fat	12%
Carbohydrates	70%
Protein	12 gm
Sodium	56 mg
Calcium	120 mg
Iron	3 mg
Dietary fiber	10 gm
Cholesterol	6 mg

EXCHANGES:

Starch/Bread	2½
Poultry/Fish/Meat	½
Vegetable	½
Fat	⅓

B L D A/S T

M Prep Time: 10-15 min.*
C Cook Time: 20 min.
Servings: 6
S Yield: (1) 7″ x 10″
baking dish

CORNMEAL-BEAN SQUARES

*¾ c. Basic Tomato Sauce (page 22)
*1½ c. cooked kidney beans or favorite beans
1¾ c. water
1 c. yellow cornmeal
3 oz. part-skim mozzarella cheese, grated
3 green bell pepper rings, halved
2 oz. chopped and seeded green chilies,
   if desired
1 c. sauteed onions, if desired

Recipe can be made ahead; it will keep covered in refrigerator for up to 5 days. Does not freeze well.

1. In a *2-c. measuring cup,* combine cornmeal with ¾ c. cold water.

2. In *1-qt. saucepan,* bring 1 c. water to a boil. Add cornmeal mixture and cook over medium-high heat, stirring constantly with a wooden spoon, for 2 to 3 minutes or until mixture becomes thickened and stiff.

3. Spray *7″ x 10″ baking dish* with nonstick coating and spoon in cornmeal mixture. Spray the back of a firm spatula with nonstick coating and use it to flatten cornmeal to an even layer.

4. Grate mozzarella cheese. Set aside.

5. In medium bowl, lightly mash beans and mix with tomato sauce. Or combine beans and tomato sauce in food processor, being careful not to over-process. Add chilies and onions, if desired.

6. Spread bean mixture evenly over cornmeal. Sprinkle with cheese and top with green pepper pieces. Refrigerate, if storing.

7. Bake in oven preheated to 350 degrees for 15 minutes or until heated thoroughly and cheese melts. Let stand 5 minutes. Cut into 6 servings, using firm spatula to lift from pan.

8. To reheat, follow Step 7. Or heat on individual serving plates for 1 to 2 minutes in microwave oven until heated thoroughly and cheese melts.

Suggestions
Serve for lunch or dinner with breadsticks and a fresh fruit salad. Because they heat up quickly, Cornmeal-Bean Squares also make a great do-ahead breakfast (omit chilies and onions).

NUTRITIONAL INFORMATION PER SERVING:

Serving size:
2¼″ x 3¼″ piece

Calories	184
Fat	14%
Carbohydrates	66%
Protein	9 gm
Sodium	71 mg
Calcium	114 mg
Iron	2 mg
Dietary fiber	4 gm
Cholesterol	8 mg

EXCHANGES:

Starch/Bread	1½
Poultry/Fish/Meat	½
Fat	½

B ☐L☐ ☐D☐ A/S T

HEALTHY BURRITOS

*1 c. cooked kidney beans
2 tsp. Mrs. Dash ®original blend seasoning
2 tb. unsalted tomato sauce
1 c. finely chopped tomato, drained of excess
    juice
1 c. finely chopped onion
1 c. finely chopped green pepper
4 oz. part-skim mozzarella cheese, grated
4 tb. reduced-fat and -calorie sour cream
2 oz. alfalfa sprouts, washed and patted dry with
    a paper towel
4 9" flour tortillas
8 toothpicks

For quick assembly, steam vegetables early in day,
cook beans ahead, mixing with sauce and seasoning.

1. Steam onions and peppers, set aside.

2. In food processor, mix beans, tomato sauce and
seasoning.

3. To assemble, spread each tortilla with ¼ bean
mixture, tomatoes, peppers and onions, mozzarella
cheese, sour cream and sprouts. Roll up and secure
with 2 toothpicks.

4. Spray *10" x 15" baking sheet* with nonstick
coating. Bake in oven preheated to 350 degrees for
8 to 10 minutes or until heated thoroughly and cheese
melts. Or heat on serving plate in microwave until
cheese melts.

Suggestions
Serve with fresh fruit and vegetable sticks.

NUTRITIONAL INFORMATION PER SERVING:	
Serving size: 1 filled burrito	
Calories	281
Fat	25%
Carbohydrates	53%
Protein	16 gm
Sodium	166 mg
Calcium	267 mg
Iron	3 mg
Dietary fiber	6 gm
Cholesterol	16 mg

EXCHANGES:	
Starch/Bread	2
Poultry/Fish/Meat	1
Vegetable	1
Fat	1

B L D A/S T

M
C
S
Prep Time: 20 min.*
Cook Time: 2-10 min.
Servings: 8
Yield: 8 halves

PITA POCKETS
Bean or Tomato

***2 c. cooked kidney or pinto beans
OR 2 c. chopped tomato, drained of excess juice
3 oz. part-skim mozzarella cheese, grated
2 c. diced carrots
2 c. diced broccoli
2 c. diced cauliflower
2 c. diced onion
4 tb. reduced-calorie and -fat mayonnaise
4 tb. nonfat yogurt
1 tb. Dijon-style mustard
4 9″ whole-wheat pitas**

Pocket stuffing can be made in advance. When ready to serve, stuff pockets and heat. (Increase baking time.)

1. Steam together vegetables.
2. Meanwhile, in small bowl mix mayonnaise, yogurt and mustard.
3. In large bowl, toss beans OR tomatoes, cheese and vegetables with mayonnaise mixture.
4. Slice pita bread in half, open pocket and fill with ⅛ of stuffing mixture. Repeat process until all pita halves are stuffed. Place on serving dish and bake in conventional oven preheated to 350 degrees for 8 to 10 minutes. Or heat in microwave oven for 2 to 5 minutes or until cheese melts.

Suggestions
Serve with Delicious Milkshakes (page 116) and sliced fresh fruit.

NUTRITIONAL INFORMATION PER SERVING:

Bean Pita Pocket

Serving size: ½ pita

Calories	201
Fat	20%
Carbohydrates	59%
Protein	11 gm
Sodium	225 mg
Calcium	159 mg
Iron	2 mg
Dietary fiber	7 gm
Cholesterol	9 mg

EXCHANGES:

Starch/Bread	1
Poultry/Fish/Meat	½
Vegetable	1½
Fat	1

Tomato Pita Pocket

Serving size: ½ pita

Calories	159
Fat	25%
Carbohydrates	57%
Protein	8 gm
Sodium	227 mg
Calcium	146 mg
Iron	1 mg
Dietary fiber	4 gm
Cholesterol	9 mg

EXCHANGES:

Starch/Bread	½
Poultry/Fish/Meat	½
Vegetable	2
Fat	¾

M   **Prep Time:** 5-10 min.
    Cook Time: 20 min.
C   (then chill)
S   **Servings:**   10
    Yield: 10 egg halves

UNDEVILED EGGS

5 large eggs
¼ c. ½%-fat cottage cheese
½ c. regular curd tofu (¼ lb.)
1 tb. reduced-calorie and -fat mayonnaise
1 tsp. Dijon-style mustard
1 tsp. parsley, plus extra for garnish
Fresh ground pepper to taste
Paprika, if desired

1. In *2-qt. saucepot,* cover eggs with water and bring to a boil. Boil gently for 15 minutes. Remove pan from heat. Immerse eggs in very cold water and let stand for 5 minutes.

2. Meanwhile, puree cottage cheese in food processor for 3 to 4 minutes or until it is the consistency of sour cream. Scrape sides often. Add tofu, mayonnaise, mustard, parsley and pepper. Puree again.

3. Peel eggs, cut lengthwise and discard yolks.

4. Fill egg-white halves with cottage cheese mixture. Garnish with parsley or paprika. Cover and chill thoroughly.

Suggestions
Serve eggs as an appetizer or combine them with muffins and fruit for a light meal.

NUTRITIONAL
INFORMATION
PER SERVING:

Serving size: ½ egg

Calories	24
Fat	35%
Carbohydrates	12%
Protein	3 gm
Sodium	33 mg
Calcium	19 mg
Iron	0 mg
Dietary fiber	0 gm
Cholesterol	1 mg

EXCHANGES:

Poultry/Fish/Meat	½
Fat	⅓

POULTRY, FISH & *Meat*

Clockwise from bottom: Salmon Filet with Healthy Topping, Stuffed Chicken Breasts with Sauce, Rice Meatballs with Sauce.

INDEX

Chicken with Parsley Sauce   76
Stuffed Chicken Breasts with Sauce   77
Breaded Chicken Breasts   78
Oven-Baked Chicken   79
Oriental Chicken   80
Chicken Vegetable Stir-Fry   81
Orange Chicken   82
Marinated Chicken   83
Suburban Chicken   84
McHealthy Chicken Nuggets   85
Quick Chicken Casserole   86
Twice-Baked Potato with Chicken   87
Your-Choice Baked Fish   88
Salmon Filet with Dill Sauce   89
Scallop or Shrimp Stir-Fry   90
Tuna or Salmon Toasts   91
Lean Shepherd's Pie   92
Lasagna with Meat Sauce   93
Meatballs with Sweet and Sour Sauce   94
Rice Meatballs with Sauce   95
Spinach Meatballs with Sauce   96

POULTRY, FISH AND MEAT

These main dishes can be the star of any show. They'll do daily service for your family—and dress up for company, too. Suburban Chicken and Salmon Filet with Dill Sauce, for instance, are perfect for weeknight meals or formal dinners.

The moderate portions of poultry, fish or meat featured in these entrees combine beautifully with vegetables, pasta and rice.

Several recipes also make great appetizers. Spinach Meatballs with Sauce, for instance, is a lean alternative to typical buffet-table fare, while McHealthy Chicken Nuggets will be a hit with the dipping crowd.

All poultry recipes call for white meat, which is lower in fat than dark meat. Turkey may be used in any chicken recipe (white meat only); the nutritional information will vary slightly.

To reduce fat, always remove skin from poultry before cooking.

Hints

- Cut raw chicken into bit-sized pieces and freeze in premeasured amounts. Defrosts quickly, or may be added to recipe while still partially frozen.
- Cook, dice, measure, label and freeze poultry for use in salads, sandwich fillings and other recipes.

Equivalents

8 oz. raw chicken = approximately 6 oz. cooked

8 oz. raw fish, shrimp or scallops = approximately 5 oz. cooked

8 oz. raw salmon = approximately 8 oz. cooked

8 oz. raw lean beef = approximately 6 oz. cooked

B L D A/S T

M **Prep Time:** 15 min.
C **Cook Time:** 20 min.
   Servings: 5
S **Yield:** 3⅓ c.

CHICKEN WITH PARSLEY SAUCE

8 oz. skinned, boned chicken breast
2 c. thinly sliced onion
2 cloves garlic, minced
¾ c. chopped fresh parsley
¼ c. water
1 c. ½%-fat cottage cheese
1½ c. skim milk
1½ tb. cornstarch
1 tb. margarine
1 tsp. low-sodium soy sauce

Recipe can be doubled. Freezes well.

1. Spray *12″ nonstick frying pan* with nonstick coating. Heat on medium and add margarine, garlic, onions and water. Cover and cook until onions are soft (about 4 to 5 minutes).

2. Meanwhile, puree cottage cheese in food processor for 3 to 4 minutes, scraping sides occasionally, until it has the consistency of sour cream.

3. Cut chicken into bite-size pieces. Uncover onion mixture, add chicken and cook slowly until chicken is almost cooked through.

4. While chicken is cooking, mix milk, cornstarch and soy sauce in *2-qt. saucepot* until well-blended. Cook on medium-high, stirring constantly with whisk, until mixture is thick and bubbly. Remove from heat and blend in cottage cheese and parsley. Pour over chicken, stirring to blend. Reduce heat to low and cook uncovered for 10 minutes. Serve or store.

Suggestions
Serve over rice, boiled new potatoes or pasta, and with Marinated Vegetables (page 56).

NUTRITIONAL
INFORMATION
PER SERVING:

Serving size: ⅔ c.
chicken and sauce

Calories	177
Fat	21%
Carbohydrates	29%
Protein	22 gm
Sodium	137 mg
Calcium	131 mg
Iron	1 mg
Dietary fiber	1 gm
Cholesterol	33 mg

EXCHANGES:

Poultry/Fish/Meat	2
Vegetable	1
Milk	½

B L D A/S T

STUFFED CHICKEN BREASTS WITH SAUCE

12 oz. skinned, boned chicken breasts (if you buy
  a 1 lb. package, use remaining chicken to
  make a stock and use meat for cold salad),
  cut into 3 oz. portions
1 c. whole-wheat bread cubes
⅔ c. thinly sliced water chestnuts
½ c. thinly sliced onion, steamed
2 tb. parsley
½ tsp. pepper
1 tsp. vegetable oil
3 tb. orange juice
8 toothpicks
¼ c. Soy-Orange Sauce (page 25)

1. Lightly pound chicken pieces on both sides
without tearing.
2. In medium bowl, mix oil, orange juice, pepper
and parsley. Add bread cubes, onion and water chestnuts. Toss until well-blended.
3. Spray *shallow baking dish* with nonstick coating.
4. Preheat oven to 375 degrees. Lay individual
pieces of chicken on flat surface. Top with ¼ stuffing
mixture, wrap chicken around and secure with
toothpicks. Place in baking dish. Repeat process for
each piece.
5. Brush pieces with ½ sauce. Bake covered for
15 minutes, baste with remaining sauce and bake
uncovered 15 minutes longer. Serve.

Suggestions
Serve with Great Boiled Potatoes (page 50), which can
be made ahead and reheated in microwave oven, and
a fresh fruit salad with Yogurt-Poppyseed Dressing
(page 43).

**NUTRITIONAL
INFORMATION
PER SERVING:**

Serving size: 1 stuffed
                  breast

Calories	205
Fat	29%
Carbohydrates	28%
Protein	22 gm
Sodium	131 mg
Calcium	34 mg
Iron	2 mg
Dietary fiber	2 gm
Cholesterol	54 mg

EXCHANGES:

Starch/Bread	½
Poultry/Fish/Meat	2
Vegetable	1½
Fat	½

B L D A/S T

M **Prep Time:** 20 min.*
Cook Time: 15 min.
C **Servings:** 6
S **Yield:** 12 oz. cooked
chicken

BREADED CHICKEN BREASTS

See Also Chicken Sandwiches (page 111)

1 lb. skinned, boned chicken breasts
*1 c. Quick Dry Bread Crumbs (page 99)
2 tb. grated parmesan cheese
1 tsp. basil
1 tsp. parsley
¾ c. ½%-fat buttermilk
1 tb. vegetable oil

Recipe can be made ahead and wrapped in serving-size portions. Or used as a filling for Chicken Sandwiches (page 111).

1. Mix bread crumbs, cheese, basil and parsley in *shallow pie pan.*
2. Pound chicken lightly on both sides.
3. Cut into manageable pieces for dipping, breading and cooking.
4. Pour buttermilk into another *shallow pie pan.*
5. Spray *12˝ nonstick frying pan* with nonstick coating. Heat on medium and add 1 tsp. oil.
6. Dip chicken pieces in buttermilk on both sides, then bread crumbs. Cook slowly until chicken is lightly browned on both sides. Add remaining oil as needed. Heat the oil before adding more chicken.
7. Warm cooked pieces in oven while cooking remaining chicken. Do not overcook. Serve or store.

Suggestions
Serve with Great Boiled Potatoes (page 50) and a tossed salad with Vinaigrette Light (page 42).

NUTRITIONAL INFORMATION PER SERVING:

Serving size: ⅙ of chicken weight

Calories	201
Fat	28%
Carbohydrates	28%
Protein	22 gm
Sodium	235 mg
Calcium	99 mg
Iron	1 mg
Dietary fiber	0 gm
Cholesterol	51 mg

EXCHANGES:

Starch/Bread	1
Poultry/Fish/Meat	2
Fat	½

B L D A/S T

M **Prep Time:** 10 min.*
C **Cook Time:** 35-40 min.
   Servings: 6
S **Yield:** 6 breast halves
   with glaze

OVEN-BAKED CHICKEN
Also Grilled Or Broiled

1½ lb. chicken breasts, halved (4 oz. each)
*¾ c. Basil-Orange Glaze (page 24)
   *OR ¾ c. Low-Sugar/Salt Basting or
   Barbeque Sauce (page 26)

Recipe doubles easily. Serve hot or cold.

   1. Remove skin from chicken, rinse and pat dry with paper towels.
   2. Preheat oven to 400 degrees. Spray *10″ x 15″ baking dish* with nonstick coating.
   3. Arrange chicken on sheet. Top with ½ of glaze.
   4. Loosely cover with foil and bake for 25 minutes. Remove foil, glaze with remaining sauce and bake uncovered for an additional 10 to 15 minutes. Serve or store.

Suggestions
Serve with Herbed Potato Sticks (page 52) or Great Boiled Potatoes (page 50), steamed vegetables and warm bread.

NUTRITIONAL INFORMATION PER SERVING:

With Orange-Basil Glaze

Serving size: 1 piece

Calories	168
Fat	18%
Carbohydrates	12%
Protein	27 gm
Sodium	63 mg
Calcium	25 mg
Iron	1 mg
Dietary fiber	0 gm
Cholesterol	72 mg

EXCHANGES:

Poultry/Fish/Meat	3

With Low-Sugar/Salt Basting/Barbeque Sauce

Serving size: 1 piece

Calories	173
Fat	22%
Carbohydrates	10%
Protein	27 gm
Sodium	69 mg
Calcium	21 mg
Iron	1 mg
Dietary fiber	0 gm
Cholesterol	72 mg

EXCHANGES:

Poultry/Fish/Meat	3
Vegetable	⅓

B L D A/S T

ORIENTAL CHICKEN

8 oz. skinned, boned chicken breast, cut into bite-size pieces
2 c. thinly sliced onions
2 large green bell peppers, cut into long, thin strips
¼ c. water
1½ c. skim milk
1½ tb. cornstarch
1½ tb. low-sodium soy sauce
1 c. ½%-fat dry curd cottage cheese
1 8-oz. can water chestnuts, drained and thinly sliced

Recipe can be doubled. Freezes well.

1. Spray *12" nonstick frying pan* with nonstick coating. Heat and add onion, green pepper and water. Cover and cook until onion and pepper are softened (3 to 5 minutes).

2. Add chicken pieces and cook slowly, uncovered, until chicken is almost cooked through.

3. Meanwhile, puree cottage cheese in food processor for 3 to 4 minutes, scraping sides often, until it has the consistency of sour cream.

4. In *2-qt. pot,* mix soy sauce, milk, and cornstarch. Cook and stir with whisk until thick and bubbly. With wooden spoon, blend in cottage cheese and chestnuts.

5. Pour over chicken mixture, stirring to blend. Simmer uncovered for 10 minutes. Serve or store.

Suggestions
Serve with Basic Rice (page 67), plain cooked rice or pasta and fresh fruit.

NUTRITIONAL INFORMATION PER SERVING:

Serving size: ¾ c. chicken and sauce

Calories	176
Fat	9%
Carbohydrates	45%
Protein	20 gm
Sodium	237 mg
Calcium	127 mg
Iron	1 mg
Dietary fiber	2 gm
Cholesterol	32 mg

EXCHANGES:

Poultry/Fish/Meat	1½
Vegetable	1½
Milk	½

B L D A/S T

M **Prep Time:** 15 min.
 Cook Time: 15 min.
C **Servings:** 4
S **Yield:** 7 c.

CHICKEN-VEGETABLE STIR-FRY

8 oz. skinned, boned chicken breast
2 c. yellow cooking onions
3 c. green beans
3 c. carrots
8 oz. can unsweetened pineapple chunks,
    drained (reserve juice)
pineapple or orange juice to bring reserved
    juice to 1 c.
1 tb. low-sodium soy sauce
1 tb. vegetable oil

Recipe is best when made fresh. Does not freeze well.

1. Dice vegetables, spray *wok or 12″ nonstick frying pan* with nonstick coating. Heat on medium.
2. Mix juice, soy sauce and oil. Add vegetables and juice mixture to heated wok. Cover and cook approximately 10 minutes or until vegetables are almost tender.
3. Meanwhile, cut chicken into bite-size pieces. When vegetables are almost tender, add chicken. Increase heat to medium-high, cooking and stirring for 3 to 5 minutes or until chicken is just cooked through.
4. Stir in pineapple chunks until heated. Serve.

Suggestions
Serve with Basic Rice (page 67), plain cooked rice or pasta, and a tossed salad.

**NUTRITIONAL
INFORMATION
PER SERVING:**

Serving size: 1¾ c.

Calories	242
Fat	20%
Carbohydrates	52%
Protein	17 gm
Sodium	261 mg
Calcium	122 mg
Iron	3 mg
Dietary fiber	8 gm
Cholesterol	36 mg

EXCHANGES:

Poultry/Fish/Meat	1½
Vegetable	3½
Fruit	⅔
Fat	½

B L D A/S T

ORANGE CHICKEN

8 oz. skinned, boned chicken breasts, cut into
    bite-size pieces
2 c. thinly sliced onion
¼ c. water
1½ c. orange juice
2 tb. cornstarch
1½ tb. low-sodium soy sauce
1 8-oz. can water chestnuts, drained and
    thinly sliced
Orange slices, if desired

Recipe can be doubled. Freezes well.

1. Spray *12" nonstick frying pan* with nonstick
coating. Heat, add onions and water and cook
covered for 3 to 5 minutes to soften onions.

2. Remove lid. Add chicken and cook slowly,
uncovered, stirring occasionally, until chicken is almost
cooked through.

3. Meanwhile, in *2-qt. saucepot,* mix orange juice,
cornstarch and soy sauce. Heat on high, stirring
constantly with a whisk, until thick and bubbly.

4. Add water chestnuts to sauce. Pour over chicken
and stir to blend.

5. Cook chicken and sauce together uncovered for
10 minutes. Serve or store.

Suggestions
Serve over rice or pasta topped with steamed
vegetables. Garnish with orange slices.

**NUTRITIONAL
INFORMATION
PER SERVING:**

Serving size: 1¼ c.
chicken and sauce

Calories	186
Fat	9%
Carbohydrates	58%
Protein	15 gm
Sodium	243 mg
Calcium	36 mg
Iron	1 mg
Dietary fiber	2 gm
Cholesterol	36 mg

EXCHANGES:

Poultry/Fish/Meat	1½
Vegetable	1½
Fruit	1

B L D A/S T

MARINATED CHICKEN STIR-FRY

**8 oz. skinned, boned chicken breast, cut into
   bite-size pieces**
½ c. Chicken or Fish Marinade (page 45)
3 c. thinly sliced yellow cooking onions
12 oz. frozen pea pods

Recipe can be doubled. Freezes well. Store in self-
sealing freezer bag and heat in microwave oven.

1. Place chicken in small bowl. Prepare marinade
and pour over chicken. Cover and refrigerate for 15
minutes.
2. Slice onions. Defrost pea pods by placing them in
large bowl and covering with hot water. Let stand 3
minutes, then drain.
3. Spray *wok or 12˝ nonstick frying pan* with
nonstick coating. Heat on medium. Drain chicken,
adding marinade to wok. Add onions. Cook covered
for 10 minutes, stirring occasionally, until almost cooked
through.
4. Remove cover and increase heat to medium-high.
Add chicken and pea pods. Cook and stir until chicken
is cooked. Serve or store.

Suggestions
Serve over rice or pasta, with Strawberry-Banana Salad
(page 40).

**NUTRITIONAL
INFORMATION
PER SERVING:**

Serving size: 1¾ c.

Calories	176
Fat	22%
Carbohydrates	40%
Protein	17 gm
Sodium	128 mg
Calcium	76 mg
Iron	3 mg
Dietary fiber	7 gm
Cholesterol	36 mg

EXCHANGES:

Poultry/Fish/Meat	1½
Vegetable	2½
Fat	½

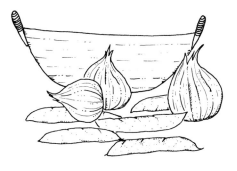

B L D A/S T

M
C Prep Time: 20 min.*
  Cook Time: 40 min.
  Servings: 8
S Yield: 8 skewers

SUBURBAN CHICKEN

½ lb. veal, cut into 16 pieces
1 lb. skinned, boned chicken breast,
    cut into 32 cubes
1 green bell pepper, cut into 16 pieces
1 red bell pepper, cut into 16 pieces
16 small whole onions
16 chunks fresh pineapple
    OR canned, unsweetened pineapple
    (20-oz. can)
½ c. ½%-fat buttermilk
*1½ c. Quick Bread Crumbs (page 99)
2 tb. parsley
½ tsp. pepper
1 tb. vegetable oil

Recipe can be assembled in advance, covered and refrigerated until ready to bake (increase baking time 5 to 10 minutes). Can be frozen after baking. Reheat loosely covered with foil so chicken does not dry out. Uncover for a few minutes to crisp.

1. Steam green pepper pieces and onions until soft enough to skewer without splitting.
2. Each *8″ metal skewer* should have 4 pieces of chicken, 2 red pepper, 2 green pepper, 2 pineapple, 2 veal and 2 onion. Assemble alternately. Repeat until all skewers are assembled.
3. Mix bread crumbs, parsley and pepper in a *shallow pie pan.*
4. Mix buttermilk and oil in another pie pan.
5. Spray *shallow baking dish* with nonstick coating. Preheat oven to 375 degrees.
6. Roll skewers in buttermilk, then bread crumbs to coat. Place in baking dish.
7. Bake 20 minutes uncovered. Turn pieces over for even browning and bake 15 minutes longer. Serve.

Suggestions
Serve with Chunky Pineapple Sauce (page 25) and Great Boiled Potatoes with Parsley (page 50).

NUTRITIONAL INFORMATION PER SERVING:

Serving size: 1 skewer

Calories	250
Fat	25%
Carbohydrates	38%
Protein	23 gm
Sodium	205 mg
Calcium	67 mg
Iron	3 mg
Dietary fiber	2 gm
Cholesterol	58 mg

EXCHANGES:

Starch/Bread	1
Poultry/Fish/Meat	2
Vegetable	1
Fruit	½
Fat	½

B | L | D | A/S | T

McHEALTHY CHICKEN NUGGETS

1 lb. skinned, boned chicken breast
*2 c. Quick Dry Bread Crumbs (page 99)
½ c. grated parmesan cheese
½ c. ½%-fat buttermilk
1 tsp. basil
1 tsp. parsley
Basic Tomato Sauce (page 22), Soy-Orange
    Sauce (page 25), Low-Sugar/Salt Basting or
    Barbeque Sauce (page 26) for dipping,
    if desired

Recipe can be prepared ahead, covered and
refrigerated until ready to bake. Or bake ahead and
serve cold or reheat.

1. Cut chicken into 48 bite-size pieces.
2. In *shallow pie pan,* mix bread crumbs, cheese,
basil and parsley. Set aside.
3. In medium bowl, mix chicken and buttermilk.
4. Preheat oven to 350 degrees. Spray *10″ x 15″
baking sheet* with nonstick coating.
5. Using slotted spoon to drain excess buttermilk,
transfer chicken pieces by spoonfuls to bread crumb
mixture. Roll until well-coated. Place pieces on baking
sheet close together but not touching. Repeat until all
chicken is coated.
6. Bake for 20 to 25 minutes. Check after 10
minutes; if bottoms are well-browned, use spatula to
turn pieces over for even browning. Do not overbake.
Check after 20 minutes.
7. Serve immediately with dipping sauce or wrap
and refrigerate for later use.

Suggestions
Serve with Potato Salad With Egg (page 31), crisp fresh
vegetable sticks and sliced fruit. Nuggets are a good
picnic item.

NUTRITIONAL INFORMATION PER SERVING:

Serving size: 6 nuggets

Calories	203
Fat	22%
Carbohydrates	39%
Protein	20 gm
Sodium	348 mg
Calcium	145 mg
Iron	2 mg
Dietary fiber	0 gm
Cholesterol	42 mg

EXCHANGES:

Starch/Bread	1
Poultry/Fish/Meat	2
Fat	½

QUICK CHICKEN CASSEROLE

*1½ c. Basic Tomato Sauce (page 22)
*2⅔ c. cooked brown rice
  8 oz. skinned, boned chicken breast
      OR 6 oz. cooked chicken
*½ c. Quick Dry Bread Crumbs (page 99)
  1 tsp. parsley
  3 oz. part-skim mozzarella cheese, grated

Recipe can be doubled or assembled ahead. Bake before freezing if chicken is raw.

1. Lightly pound raw chicken pieces on both sides. Cut into bite-size pieces for even distribution in casserole. If using cooked chicken, cut into bite-size pieces but do not pound.

2. Spray *9" to 10" casserole* with nonstick coating. Casserole should be at least 3" tall.

3. Mix bread crumbs with parsley.

4. Spread ½ c. tomato sauce on bottom of casserole. Distribute evenly in layers, rice, chicken pieces, bread crumbs and cheese. Drizzle with remaining sauce.

5. Bake covered in oven preheated to 350 degrees for 20 minutes. Or bake, partially covered, in microwave oven on medium-high heat for 5 minutes, then on high for 3 minutes. If using cooked chicken, bake until heated thoroughly and cheese melts.

Suggestions
Serve with Delightful Fruit Salad (page 39).

**NUTRITIONAL
INFORMATION
PER SERVING:**

Serving size:
¼ casserole

Calories	366
Fat	16%
Carbohydrates	56%
Protein	25 gm
Sodium	233 mg
Calcium	188 mg
Iron	3 mg
Dietary fiber	5 gm
Cholesterol	48 mg

EXCHANGES:

Starch/Bread	2½
Poultry/Fish/Meat	2
Vegetable	½
Fat	½

B [L] [D] A/S [T]

[M]
[C]
Prep Time: 15 min.
Cook Time: 20 min. -
1 hr.
S **Servings:**   2
   Yield: 2 potatoes

TWICE-BAKED POTATO WITH CHICKEN

See Also Twice-Baked Potatoes (page 62)

2 large baking potatoes, scrubbed (7-8 oz. each)
½ c. frozen peas
½ c. diced onion
1 tb. vegetable oil
1½ tb. grated parmesan cheese
1 tsp. chives
3 oz. raw diced chicken breast
      OR ½ c. diced, cooked chicken breast
freshly ground pepper to taste

Prepare ahead in any quantity. Cover and refrigerate or wrap individually and freeze. To serve, defrost and heat through. Or remove from freezer in morning and heat in microwave oven at lunchtime.

1. Bake potatoes at 400 degrees for 45 to 50 minutes. (To speed baking, prebake in microwave oven but bake the last 15 minutes in conventional oven to crisp potato skins.)

2. While potatoes are baking, place raw chicken in *small stock pot,* cover with water and simmer, partially covered, for 10-12 minutes. If using cooked chicken, skip this step.

3. Steam onions. Set aside.

4. In a small bowl, cover peas with hot water and let stand for 2 minutes. Drain and set aside.

5. Remove potatoes from oven and let cook for 5 minutes for easier handling. Holding potato with pot-holder, slice lengthwise to remove top quarter. With small spoon, gently scoop pulp from top and bottom skins, being careful not to break them. Reserve skins.

6. In medium bowl, lightly mash potato pulp with a fork. Mix in parmesan cheese, oil, chives and pepper. When well-blended, mix in chicken and vegetables.

7. Stuff potato mixture back into skins. They will be very full. Put potato tops in place. Return to oven and heat thoroughly, or cover and refrigerate or freeze.

Suggestions
Serve with Healthy Topping (page 26) and a tossed salad.

NUTRITIONAL INFORMATION PER SERVING:

Serving size: 1 stuffed potato

Calories	391
Fat	22%
Carbohydrates	60%
Protein	18 gm
Sodium	160 mg
Calcium	109 mg
Iron	4 mg
Dietary fiber	7 gm
Cholesterol	28 mg

EXCHANGES:

Starch/Bread	3¼
Poultry/Fish/Meat	1
Vegetable	½
Fat	1½

B ☐L☐ ☐D☐ A/S T

M
C
S
Prep Time: 15 min.*
Cook Time: 12-20 min.
Servings: 4
Yield: 20 oz. fish
with sauce

YOUR CHOICE BAKED FISH
Also Grilled Or Broiled

2 lb. Orange Roughy
OR fish of choice
***1 c. Basic Tomato Sauce (page 22)**
OR ½ c. Parsley-Orange Sauce (page 24)
OR ½ c. Soy-Orange Sauce (page 25)

Recipe is quick if using either orange sauces, which can be made in a few minutes. Basic Tomato Sauce can be made ahead and frozen in 1-c. serving size.

1. Rinse fish and pat dry with paper towels.
2. Prepare Parsley-Orange Sauce or Soy-Orange Sauce.
3. Preheat oven to 325 degrees. Spray *shallow baking dish* with nonstick coating. Use baking dish large enough that fish pieces will not overlap.
4. Arrange pieces on dish. Top with sauce and bake for 12 to 20 minutes, depending on thickness of fish. Check after 12 minutes. Fish should flake with a fork when done. Serve immediately.

Suggestions
Serve with Basic Rice (page 67), crisp vegetable sticks or Marinated Vegetables (page 56) and Oat Bran Muffins (page 101).

NUTRITIONAL INFORMATION PER SERVING:
(Based on Orange Roughy)

With Parsley-Orange Sauce

Serving size: 5 oz. cooked fish with sauce

Calories	165
Fat	15%
Carbohydrates	15%
Protein	22 gm
Sodium	24 mg
Calcium	8 mg
Iron	0 mg
Dietary fiber	0 gm
Cholesterol	0 mg

EXCHANGES:

Poultry/Fish/Meat	2
Fruit	½
Fat	½

With Soy-Orange Sauce

Serving size: 5 oz. cooked fish with sauce

Calories	164
Fat	18%
Carbohydrates	20%
Protein	22 gm
Sodium	183 mg
Calcium	5 mg
Iron	0 mg
Dietary fiber	0 gm
Cholesterol	0 mg

EXCHANGES:

Poultry/Fish/Meat	2
Fruit	½
Fat	½

B L |D| A/S T

M **Prep Time:** 5 min.
   Cook Time: 20-25 min.
C **Servings:** 4
S **Yield:** 1 lb. salmon

SALMON FILET WITH HEALTHY TOPPING

---

1 lb. salmon filets
½ c. Healthy Topping (page 26) with dill

1. Spray *9" x 13" baking pan* with nonstick coating. Preheat oven to 325 degrees.
2. Place salmon skin side down in baking dish. Spread ½ the sauce on top and bake for 20 to 25 minutes or until fish flakes with a fork. Serve with remaining sauce, if desired.

Suggestions
Serve with Basic Rice (page 67) and a salad of spinach, croutons, red onions and Lemon-Orange Dressing (page 44).

NUTRITIONAL INFORMATION PER SERVING:

Serving size: 4 oz. salmon with sauce

Calories	152
Fat	27%
Carbohydrates	2%
Protein	26 gm
Sodium	7 mg
Calcium	13 mg
Iron	0 mg
Dietary fiber	0 gm
Cholesterol	1 mg

EXCHANGES:

Poultry/Fish/Meat	2

B . L D A/S T

Prep Time: 15 min.
Cook Time: 15 min.
Servings: 4
Yield: 4 c.
M
C
S

SCALLOP OR SHRIMP STIR-FRY

1 lb. bay scallops, drained and rinsed
  OR 1 lb. cleaned, raw shrimp, rinsed
    (18-20 oz. with shells)
¼ c. dry white wine
1 tb. margarine
1 c. canned unsalted tomatoes, seeded, drained
  and chopped
2 tb. chopped green onion
1½ c. thinly sliced yellow bell pepper (1 large)
  or green bell pepper
1 c. sliced fresh mushrooms
½ tsp. basil
2-3 tsp. cornstarch, if desired

1. Over medium-high heat, melt margarine in *wok or 12" nonstick frying pan.* Add wine and all vegetables except onion. Cook and stir until vegetables are tender but still firm (about 3 to 5 minutes). If there is excess liquid from green peppers, thicken by removing several tablespoons of liquid and blending with cornstarch in small container. Return mixture to wok, cooking and stirring to thicken. Proceed with Step 2.
2. Add scallops or shrimp, basil and onions. Cook and stir until scallops are opaque or shrimp is pink and firm (about 3 to 4 minutes). Do not overcook. Serve immediately.

Suggestions
Serve with Basic Rice with added wild rice (page 67) and a fresh fruit salad with Lemon-Orange Dressing (page 44).

NUTRITIONAL INFORMATION PER SERVING:

With Scallops

Serving size: 1 c.

Calories	149
Fat	21%
Carbohydrates	23%
Protein	18 gm
Sodium	328 mg
Calcium	43 mg
Iron	3 mg
Dietary fiber	2 gm
Cholesterol	37 mg

EXCHANGES:

Poultry/Fish/Meat	2
Vegetable	1
Fat	Tr

With Shrimp

Serving size: 1 c.

Calories	160
Fat	23%
Carbohydrates	16%
Protein	22 gm
Sodium	198 mg
Calcium	85 mg
Iron	3 mg
Dietary fiber	2 gm
Cholesterol	162 mg

EXCHANGES:

Poultry/Fish/Meat	2
Vegetable	1
Fat	½

B ☐L☐ ☐D☐ ☐A/S☐ T

Prep Time: 15 min.
Cook Time: 5 min.
Servings: 4
Yield: 8 slices bread
with 2⅔ c. topping

TUNA OR SALMON TOASTS

1 6½-oz. can water-packed tuna, drained
    OR 1 6½-oz. can water-packed salmon,
        drained
½ c. finely chopped green pepper
¼ c. finely chopped green onion
2 oz. part-skim mozzarella cheese, cut into
    very small pieces
4-oz. can mushroom pieces, drained and
    finely chopped
½ c. finely chopped water chestnuts
¼ c. ½%-fat dry curd cottage cheese
½ tsp. lemon juice
2 tb. low-fat mayonnaise
2 tb. nonfat yogurt
1½ tsp. Mrs. Dash® lemon-and-herb seasoning
8 slices whole-wheat bread, lightly toasted

1. In medium bowl, flake tuna or salmon with fork to break apart. Add green pepper, onion, mozzarella, mushrooms and chestnuts.
2. In food processor, puree cottage cheese until smooth, scraping sides occasionally. Add lemon juice, mayonnaise and seasoning. Puree again until well-blended.
3. Toss tuna or salmon with dressing. Place ⅛ of mixture on each slice of toast and spread to edges. Broil until cheese melts and mixture is warmed through. Serve immediately.

Suggestions
Serve with fresh fruit and ½ Delicious Milkshake of choice (page 116).
    For appetizers; cut each piece of bread in thirds. Makes 24.

NUTRITIONAL INFORMATION PER SERVING:

Tuna Toasts

Serving size: 2 slices with ⅔ c. topping

Calories	276
Fat	24%
Carbohydrates	42%
Protein	24 gm
Sodium	551 mg
Calcium	149 mg
Iron	3 mg
Dietary fiber	5 gm
Cholesterol	28 mg

EXCHANGES:

Starch/Bread	2
Poultry/Fish/Meat	1½
Vegetable	½
Fat	¾

Salmon Toasts

Serving size: 2 slices with ⅔ c. topping

Calories	282
Fat	29%
Carbohydrates	42%
Protein	20 gm
Sodium	623 mg
Calcium	237 mg
Iron	3 mg
Dietary fiber	5 gm
Cholesterol	30 mg

EXCHANGES:

Starch/Bread	2
Poultry/Fish/Meat	2
Vegetable	½
Fat	1

B ☐L☐ ☐D☐ A/S ☐T☐

M **Prep Time:** 20 min.
C **Cook Time:** 45 min.
  Servings: 8
S **Yield:** 9″ x 13″ pan

LEAN SHEPHERD'S PIE
See Also Meatless Shepherd's Pie
(page 61)

FILLING
1 lb. lean ground round
1 15-oz. can unsalted tomato sauce
1 c. chopped onion
1 garlic clove, chopped
1 tsp. each basil and oregano
½ tsp. pepper
2 c. diced carrots, fresh or frozen
2 c. diced broccoli, fresh or frozen
2 c. diced cauliflower, fresh or frozen

TOPPING
10 c. peeled and diced potatoes (approx. 3¾ lbs.)
1 whole medium onion, skinned
2 tsp. oregano
½ tsp. pepper
½ c. ½%-fat cottage cheese
2 tb. grated parmesan cheese
2 tb. ½%-fat buttermilk (more, if necessary)
1 medium tomato, sliced, if desired

NUTRITIONAL INFORMATION PER SERVING:

Serving size:
⅛ 9″ x 13″ pan or
¼ 9″ pan

Calories	353
Fat	9%
Carbohydrates	65%
Protein	23 gm
Sodium	113 mg
Calcium	113 mg
Iron	3 mg
Dietary fiber	7 gm
Cholesterol	36 mg

EXCHANGES:

Starch/Bread	2½
Poultry/Fish/Meat	1½
Vegetable	1½
Fat	½

Recipe freezes well. Can be made ahead in *2 9″ round pans* (4 servings each). Eat one, freeze one. Heat in conventional oven as microwave changes potato consistency.

1. Steam carrots, broccoli and cauliflower until tender, set aside.

2. In *12″ nonstick frying pan,* cook meat and onion on medium-high, stirring frequently to break up meat and cook onion evenly. After meat has browned, drain in colander to remove excess fat. Return to pan. Add remaining filling ingredients, stirring to blend. Place mixture in *one 9″ x 13″ baking dish or two 9″ round baking dishes* that have been sprayed with nonstick coating.

3. Meanwhile, combine diced potatoes and whole onion in *6-qt. stock pot.* Cover with water and bring to a boil. Cook partially covered until potatoes are soft enough to mash (about 20 minutes).

4. While potatoes are cooking, puree cottage cheese in food processor for 3 to 4 minutes, scraping sides occasionally, until it is the consistency of sour cream.

5. Drain cooked potatoes in colander, discarding onion, and return to pot. Add buttermilk and mash with hand masher or electric mixer. Do not overbeat. Stir in spices, cottage cheese and parmesan cheese.

6. Top filling with potato mixture and smooth to edges with spatula. Garnish with tomato slices.

7. In oven preheated to 350 degrees, bake 15 minutes or until thoroughly heated and top is slightly browned. Serve. Or freeze unbaked.

Suggestions
Serve with a large tossed salad and bread sticks.

B L D A/S T

C
S

Prep Time: 20 min.*
Cook Time: 40 min.
Servings: 4
Yield: (1) 8″ x 8″ pan

LASAGNA WITH MEAT SAUCE

See Also Tofu Lasagna (page 64)

*2½ c. Spaghetti Sauce with Meat (page 20),
   warmed
3 c. diced red and green bell peppers
1 c. chopped onion
4 oz. part-skim mozzarella cheese, grated
4 oz. canned mushrooms, drained
½-lb. package lasagna noodles
4 oz. part-skim riccota cheese

Recipe can be doubled and assembled in *9″ x 13″
baking pan.* Freezes well.

1. Cook lasagna noodles according to package
directions.
2. Meanwhile, steam green peppers and onions.
3. Preheat oven to 350 degrees. Spray *8″ x 8″
baking pan* with nonstick coating.
4. Place ½ c. sauce on bottom of pan. Layer
lasagna noodles, mushrooms, peppers, onion, riccota
cheese, mozzarella cheese and 1 c. sauce. Repeat.
5. Bake uncovered for 25 minutes. Remove from
oven and let stand 10 minutes. Cut and serve.

Suggestions
Serve with Crusty Continental Bread (page 108) and
a tossed salad.

**NUTRITIONAL
INFORMATION
PER SERVING:**

Serving size:
4″ x 4″ square

Calories	334
Fat	29%
Carbohydrates	45%
Protein	23 gm
Sodium	230 mg
Calcium	340 mg
Iron	5 mg
Dietary fiber	4 gm
Cholesterol	42 mg

EXCHANGES:

Starch/Bread	1
Poultry/Fish/Meat	2
Vegetable	3
Fat	1

Poultry, Fish and Meat   93

B L D A/S T

M
C
S

Prep Time: 20 min.
Cook Time: 55 min.
Servings: 5
Yield: 10 meatballs

MEATBALLS WITH SWEET & SOUR SAUCE

MEATBALLS

½ lb. lean ground round
½ c. old-fashioned oats
1 egg white
½ c. finely chopped green onion
8-oz. can mushrooms, drained and
    finely chopped
2 tb. skim milk
1 tsp. low-sodium soy sauce
½ tsp. freshly ground pepper

SAUCE

½ c. unsweetened crushed pineapple, drained
    (reserve juice)
Enough pineapple juice to bring reserved juice
    to 1 c.
2 tb. cider vinegar
2 tsp. low-sodium soy sauce
2½ tb. cornstarch
1 c. Basic Chicken or Beef Stock (pages 7)
    or water
¾ c. finely chopped green bell pepper

NUTRITIONAL INFORMATION PER SERVING:

Serving size:
2 meatballs with sauce

Calories	153
Fat	15%
Carbohydrates	48%
Protein	14 gm
Sodium	81 mg
Calcium	24 mg
Iron	2 mg
Dietary fiber	2 gm
Cholesterol	28 mg

EXCHANGES:

Poultry/Fish/Meat	1½
Vegetable	½
Fruit	½

Recipe can be doubled. Freezes well. Eat one, freeze one.

1. In large bowl, beat egg white with fork. Add all meatball ingredients and mix until well-blended.

2. Spray *10″ x 15″ nonstick baking sheet* with nonstick coating. Preheat oven to 375 degrees.

3. By hand, roll meat into 10 meatballs. Arrange 1″ apart on baking sheet. Bake for 35 minutes.

4. While meatballs are baking, prepare sauce.

5. Remove meatballs from oven and let stand for 10 minutes before adding to sauce.

6. In *3-qt. stock pot,* blend well pineapple juice, vinegar, soy sauce, cornstarch and stock or water. Heat on high, stirring constantly, until sauce is thick and bubbly and becomes clear. Add pineapple and green pepper, cook 2 minutes longer.

7. Gently stir meatballs into sauce. Heat together 10 minutes. Serve or store.

Suggestions

Serve over rice or pasta with a tossed salad with Vinaigrette, Regular (page 42) and Oat Bran Muffins (page 101). For an appetizer, make into 20 smaller meatballs and bake for 25 minutes. Let stand 10 minutes, then cover with ½ sauce.

B L D A/S T

M
C
S
Prep Time: 15 min.*
Cook Time: 55 min.
Servings: 6
Yield: 12 meatballs

RICE MEATBALLS WITH SAUCE

*3½ c. Basic Tomato Sauce (page 22)
*¾ c. cooked brown rice
 ½ lb. lean ground beef
 8-oz. can water chestnuts, drained and diced
 ½ c. finely chopped green onion
 1 egg white
 2 tb. skim milk
 1 tb. parsley

Recipe can be doubled. Freezes well. If preparing
Basic Tomato Sauce, start first and increase prep time
by 10 minutes.

1. In large bowl, beat egg white with fork. Add all
ingredients except Basic Tomato Sauce, blending well.

2. Spray *10" x 15" nonstick baking sheet* with
nonstick coating. Preheat oven to 350 degrees.

3. By hand, roll meat into 12 meatballs. Arrange
1" apart on baking sheet. Bake for 35 minutes or until
well-browned.

4. While meatballs are baking, warm sauce.

5. Remove meatballs from oven and let stand for
10 minutes before adding to sauce.

6. Gently stir meatballs into warm sauce and simmer
together for 10 minutes. Serve or store.

Suggestions
Serve over pasta with a large tossed salad and bread.
For an appetizer, make into 24 smaller meatballs and
bake for 25 minutes. Let stand 10 minutes then cover
with 1½ c. sauce.

**NUTRITIONAL
INFORMATION
PER SERVING:**

Serving size:
2 meatballs with sauce

Calories	232
Fat	10%
Carbohydrates	66%
Protein	14 gm
Sodium	46 mg
Calcium	42 mg
Iron	3 mg
Dietary fiber	3 gm
Cholesterol	23 mg

EXCHANGES:

Starch/Bread	½
Poultry/Fish/Meat	1
Vegetable	2½
Fat	1

B | L | D | A/S | T

Prep Time: 15 min.*
Cook Time: 1 hr.
Servings: 5
Yield: 10 meatballs

M
C
S

SPINACH MEATBALLS WITH SAUCE

*3½ c. Basic Tomato Sauce (page 22)
*1 10-oz. pkg. frozen chopped spinach, defrosted,
    drained and squeezed dry
½ lb. lean ground round
1 green onion, finely chopped
2 tb. grated parmesan cheese
¼ c. dry bread crumbs
1 egg white
¼ c. skim milk
1 tsp. basil
¼ tsp. pepper

Recipe can be doubled. Freezes well. If preparing
Basic Tomato Sauce, start first and increase prep time
by 10 minutes.

1. In large bowl, beat egg white with fork. Add all
ingredients except Basic Tomato Sauce, blending well.

2. Spray *10" x 15" nonstick baking sheet* with
nonstick coating. Preheat oven to 375 degrees.

3. By hand, roll meat into 10 meatballs. Arrange
1" apart on baking sheet.

4. Bake for 40 minutes. Warm sauce while meatballs
are baking. Remove meatballs from oven and let stand
10 minutes before adding to sauce.

5. Gently stir meatballs into sauce, cooking together
for 10 minutes. Serve or store.

Suggestions

Serve over rice with warm bread and sliced fresh fruit.
For an appetizer, make into 20 smaller meatballs and
bake for 25 minutes. Let stand 10 minutes, then cover
with 1½ c. sauce.

NUTRITIONAL INFORMATION PER SERVING:

Serving size:
2 meatballs with sauce

Calories	187
Fat	16%
Carbohydrates	46%
Protein	18 gm
Sodium	187 mg
Calcium	168 mg
Iron	4 mg
Dietary fiber	2 gm
Cholesterol	30 mg

EXCHANGES:

Poultry/Fish/Meat	1½
Vegetable	1½
Fat	½

GRAINS
& Fillings

Clockwise from bottom: Pizza, Oat Bran Muffins, Healthy Bread Your Family Will Love, Crusty Continental Bread.

INDEX

Banana Bread   100
Oat Bran Muffins   101
Oats & Fruit Breakfast   102
Wheat & Fruit Breakfast   103
Pancakes   104
Unconventional French Toast   105
White Bread   106
Healthy Bread Your Family Will Love   107
Crusty Continental Bread   108
Pizza   109
Tuna or Shrimp Spread   110
Chicken Spread   111
Chicken Sandwiches   111
No-Yolk Egg Salad   112

Remember the commercial that said, "It fills you up, not out!"? That's the whole truth about grains.

Grains not only contain many essential minerals and vitamins, they are a major source of energy. And ounce for ounce, grains contain about half as many calories as fats do.

So, go ahead. Indulge in pancakes on a weekend morning. Treat yourself to banana bread—or pizza made from Crusty Continental Bread. The grains these recipes contain make these foods delicious *and* healthy.

Fast meals, snacks and travelers

- Spread 2 tb. dry-curd cottage cheese or part-skim ricotta cheese on Healthy Bread Your Family Will Love. Top with 2 tsp. fruit conserve and broil.
- Top a piece of whole-grain bread with 1½ tb. Healthy Topping and broil.
- On a flour tortilla, spread 1 tb. peanut butter. Add 1 tb. fruit conserve or sprinkle with raisins. Roll up and wrap in plastic wrap. Peel down plastic wrap to eat. (Kids love this one!)
- Frozen pizza: Pack directly from the freezer in the morning and heat in a microwave oven at work for lunch.
- Combine 3 c. air-popped, unsalted popcorn with 2 tb. raisins and ⅛ c. dry-roasted, unsalted peanuts in a plastic bag. Keep in your car, desk or purse for a quick snack.

Quick bread crumbs

To make soft bread crumbs, tear slices of fresh bread into pieces and shred them in a food processor or blender (process one slice at a time). Crumbs can be frozen.

4 slices fresh bread = approximately 1½ c. soft bread crumbs

Use stale bread and the same process to make dry bread crumbs. The texture will be finer than that of soft bread crumbs.

4 slices stale bread = approximately 1¼ c. dry bread crumbs

Making croutons

Dice bread and place on baking sheet that has been sprayed with nonstick coating. Bake at 325 degrees until cubes are crisp (about 15 minutes). Meanwhile, shake into a plastic bag paprika, parsley or herb of choice. Parmesan cheese may be used, but sodium and fat content will increase. Remove croutons from oven, add to bag and shake to coat. Let cool and store in air-tight container or freeze.

Hint

- During baking preparation, use a large measuring cup as one of the bowls to save clean-up time.

Prep Time: 15 min.
Cook Time: 35-40 min.
Servings: 14
Yield: 1 loaf

BANANA BREAD

2 c. unbleached all-purpose flour
½ tsp. baking soda
2 tsp. baking powder
½ tsp. nutmeg
½ tsp. cinnamon
½ c. chopped golden raisins
2 tb. grated orange or lemon rind
2 tb. frozen orange juice concentrate
¼ c. vegetable oil
2 egg whites
1¼ c. pureed ripe banana

Recipe can be doubled and freezes well. Slice before freezing so individual slices can be removed if desired. Banana Bread can be toasted.

1. In large bowl, combine dry ingredients. Set aside.
2. Puree banana in a food processor or blender. Reserve extra and freeze in a labeled container.
3. In small bowl, beat egg whites with a fork. Blend in oil and orange juice concentrate. Add pureed bananas, blend again. Add moist ingredients to dry mixture, stirring to blend. Do not overbeat.
4. Preheat oven to 325 degrees, spray *9″ x 5″ nonstick bread pan* with nonstick coating. Pour mixture into pan and bake for 35 to 40 minutes. Remove from pan and cool on wire rack. Serve or store.

Suggestions
Banana Bread can be served for dessert or as an accompaniment to a main dish salad.

NUTRITIONAL INFORMATION PER SERVING:

Serving size: 1 slice

Calories	129
Fat	29%
Carbohydrates	63%
Protein	3 gm
Sodium	86 mg
Calcium	17 mg
Iron	1 mg
Dietary fiber	1 gm
Cholesterol	0 mg

EXCHANGES:

Starch/Bread	1
Fruit	½
Fat	½

OAT BRAN MUFFINS

1 c. oat bran
1 c. unbleached all-purpose flour
2 tsp. baking powder
2 tb. grated orange rind
½ c. finely chopped golden raisins
    OR ½ c. finely chopped apricots
    OR ½ c. finely chopped dates
    OR ¾ c. fresh or frozen unsweetened
       blueberries
½ c. ½%-fat buttermilk
1 egg white
2 tb. vegetable oil
¼ c. raspberry, orange or peach conserve
¼ c. frozen orange juice concentrate

Recipe doubles well. Muffins are best when served fresh but can be frozen. Do-ahead preparation: follow step 1, covering measuring cup and refrigerating. At baking time, proceed with Step 2. If preparing Oat Bran Muffins With Blueberries, use fruit directly from freezer, breaking apart before adding to batter.

1. Mix first 4 ingredients in medium bowl. Set aside. In *2-c. measuring cup,* combine remaining ingredients (except fruit) and blend with fork until smooth.
2. Mix together wet and dry ingredients. Fold in fruit.
3. Preheat oven to 400 degrees. Spray *12-c. muffin pan (2¾″ cups)* with nonstick coating. Fill cups evenly and bake for 17 to 18 minutes. Remove from pan and serve or cool and store.

Suggestions
For a great breakfast, serve with Delicious Milkshakes (pages 116-119). Muffins are a good accompaniment for most meals.

**NUTRITIONAL
INFORMATION
PER SERVING:**

Serving size: 1 muffin

Calories	170
Fat	22%
Carbohydrates	67%
Protein	5 gm
Sodium	72 mg
Calcium	37 mg
Iron	1 mg
Dietary fiber	3 gm
Cholesterol	0 mg

EXCHANGES:

Starch/Bread	1½
Fruit	½
Fat	1

OATS & FRUIT BREAKFAST

¼ c. old-fashioned oats
¼ c. oat bran
2 tb. raisins
¼ c. diced apple
¾ c. water
¼ tsp. cinnamon (or to taste)
1 walnut, broken
½ c. skim milk

Recipe can be doubled.

1. Combine all ingredients except milk in a *2-c. to 1-qt. pot* and bring to a boil. Boil 1 minute, stirring often.
2. Remove from heat, cover and let stand for 5 minutes. Serve with ½ c. milk.

Suggestions
Slice remaining apple to eat with cereal.

**NUTRITIONAL
INFORMATION
PER SERVING:**

Serving size: 1 c.

Calories	318
Fat	16%
Carbohydrates	70%
Protein	11 gm
Sodium	68 mg
Calcium	195 mg
Iron	3 mg
Dietary fiber	3 gm
Cholesterol	2 mg

EXCHANGES:

Starch/Bread	1½
Fruit	1½
Milk	½
Fat	1½

M
C
S

Prep Time: 2 min.
Cook Time: 5 min.
Servings: 1
Yield: 1⅓ c.

WHEAT & FRUIT BREAKFAST

2½ tb. quick-cooking wheat cereal
1 tb. oat bran
2 tb. golden raisins
1 whole walnut, broken
1⅓ c. skim milk

1. Heat milk until almost boiling in a *2-c. to 1-qt. pot,* stirring with a whisk so it does not burn. Or, heat milk in *2-c. glass measuring cup* in microwave oven and pour into pot to continue cooking.
2. Add cereal and oat bran to milk. Cook and stir 2 to 3 minutes, or until mixture is thick and bubbly.
3. Add remaining ingredients. Serve.

Suggestions
Serve with sliced, fresh fruit.

**NUTRITIONAL
INFORMATION
PER SERVING:**

Serving size: 1⅓ c.

Calories	295
Fat	19%
Carbohydrates	61%
Protein	15 gm
Sodium	168 mg
Calcium	425 mg
Iron	3 mg
Dietary fiber	3 gm
Cholesterol	5 mg

EXCHANGES:

Starch/Bread	1
Fruit	1
Milk	1⅓
Fat	1

B L D A/S T

M **Prep Time:** 5-10 min.
Cook Time: 5-8 min.
C **Servings:** 6
S **Yield:** 12 pancakes

PANCAKES
Plain or Blueberry

PLAIN
1 c. unbleached all-purpose flour
1 tb. baking powder
¼ c. raspberry, orange or peach conserve
2 egg whites
1 tb. vegetable oil
⅔ c. skim milk
Conserve for topping, if desired

BLUEBERRY
Above ingredients
Decrease conserve to 1 tb.
¾ c. fresh or frozen blueberries
Blueberry conserve for topping, if desired

Recipe can be easily doubled and frozen in batches. To freeze, lay pancakes flat on cookie sheet, freeze and transfer to a freezer bag. Reheat in toaster.

1. In medium bowl, mix together flour and baking powder.

2. Spray *nonstick griddle or frying pan* with nonstick coating and heat.

3. In small bowl, beat egg whites with a fork. Add remaining ingredients and blend well.

4. Combine wet and dry ingredients. Pour or scoop onto griddle to make 3½" rounds. Turn when top bubbles and the edge is dry. Cook other side.
Serve or store.

Note: If using blueberry conserve, avoid adding it to batter; it will color pancakes blue.

Suggestions
Pancakes make a fast breakfast when done ahead and frozen. They are also good as a snack.

NUTRITIONAL INFORMATION PER SERVING:

Plain Pancakes

Serving size: 2 pancakes

Calories	124
Fat	20%
Carbohydrates	66%
Protein	4 gm
Sodium	195 mg
Calcium	131 mg
Iron	1 mg
Dietary fiber	1 gm
Cholesterol	0 mg

EXCHANGES:

Starch/Bread	1
Poultry/Fish/Meat	⅕
Fat	½

Blueberry Pancakes

Serving size: 2 pancakes

Calories	135
Fat	19%
Carbohydrates	67%
Protein	4 gm
Sodium	195 mg
Calcium	129 mg
Iron	1 mg
Dietary fiber	1 gm
Cholesterol	0 mg

EXCHANGES:

Starch/Bread	1
Poultry/Fish/Meat	⅕
Fruit	⅕
Fat	½

UNCONVENTIONAL FRENCH TOAST

8 slices whole-grain bread or Healthy Bread Your Family Will Love (page 107)
3 egg whites
½ c. nonfat yogurt
¾ tsp. cinnamon
¼ tsp. nutmeg
2 tsp. vegetable oil

A more complete breakfast than plain toast and less fat than regular french toast. Recipe can be made ahead, frozen and reheated in toaster or toaster oven.

1. In small bowl, combine egg whites, yogurt, spices and oil. Beat with a fork.
2. Spray *nonstick pan or griddle* with nonstick coating and heat.
3. Spread mixture on one side of bread slice. Place face down on hot griddle. Continue until all pieces are coated. Spread remaining mixture on tops of bread. Turn when browned and cook other side. Serve or store. After bread has cooled, wrap individually and freeze.

Suggestions
Serve with conserve of choice and a piece of fruit. For a breakfast that travels well, spread conserve between 2 pieces of french toast and wrap in foil. (Use foil as a holder.)

NUTRITIONAL INFORMATION PER SERVING:

Serving size: 2 pieces

Calories	168
Fat	23%
Carbohydrates	57%
Protein	9 gm
Sodium	366 mg
Calcium	100 mg
Iron	2 mg
Dietary fiber	5 gm
Cholesterol	1 mg

EXCHANGES:

Starch/Bread	2
Poultry/Fish/Meat	½
Milk	Tr
Fat	½

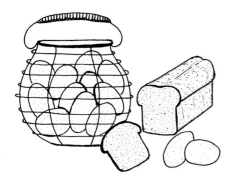

M **Prep Time:** 15 min.
          (plus rising)
C **Cook Time:** 45 min.
S **Servings:** 28
   Yield: 2 loaves

WHITE BREAD

5½ c. unbleached all-purpose flour
½ c. powdered milk
2 pkgs. dry yeast
1 tb. sugar
1 tsp. salt
2 tb. vegetable oil
2 c. water

Recipe freezes well. Slice before freezing so individual slices can be removed from freezer if desired.

1. In large mixing bowl, combine 3 c. flour, milk, yeast, sugar and salt.

2. In *1-qt. stock pot,* heat water and oil until warm (120 to 130 degrees), not hot. Add to flour mixture and beat 3 minutes with electric mixer at medium speed. With wooden spoon, gradually stir in enough remaining flour to make a firm dough. Turn onto floured surface and knead until smooth and elastic (about 5 to 8 minutes).

3. Spray a large bowl and *2 9″ x 5″ baking pans* with nonstick coating. Place dough in bowl and turn to coat top. Cover and let rise in a warm place until doubled (about 1 hour).

4. Punch down dough. Divide into 2 pieces. On lightly floured surface, roll or pat each piece into a 14″ x 7″rectangle. Starting with the short end, tightly roll up the first piece. Pinch edges and ends to seal. Place in pan. Repeat. Cover and let rise in warm place until doubled (about 45 minutes). Bake in oven preheated to 350 degrees for 45 minutes. Remove from pans, cool on wire rack.

Suggestions
Makes a classic traveling lunch when teamed with peanut butter (try the peanuts only type: no sugar or salt added) and conserve. This all-purpose bread is great for sandwiches, toast, bread crumbs and croutons.

**NUTRITIONAL
INFORMATION
PER SERVING:**

Serving size: 1 slice

Calories	99
Fat	11%
Carbohydrates	77%
Protein	3 gm
Sodium	77 mg
Calcium	19 mg
Iron	1 mg
Dietary fiber	1 gm
Cholesterol	0 mg

EXCHANGES:

Starch/Bread	1
Fat	¼

B L D A/S T

HEALTHY BREAD
YOUR FAMILY WILL LOVE

1 c. whole-wheat flour
3½ c. - 4 c. unbleached all-purpose flour
½ c. wheat germ
2 pkgs. dry yeast
1 tb. sugar
1 tsp. salt
2 c. water
3 tb. vegetable oil

Recipe freezes well. Slice before freezing so individual slices can be removed from freezer if desired.

1. In large mixing bowl, combine 2 c. white flour, whole-wheat flour, wheat germ, sugar, salt and yeast.

2. In *1-qt. stock pot,* heat water and oil until warm (120-130 degrees), not hot. Add to flour mixture and beat 3 minutes with electric mixer at medium speed. With wooden spoon, gradually add enough remaining flour to make a firm dough. Turn onto floured surface and knead until smooth and elastic (about 5 to 8 minutes).

3. Spray a large bowl and *2 9″ x 5″ baking pans* with nonstick coating. Place dough in bowl and turn to coat top. Cover and let rise in warm place until doubled (about 1 hour).

4. Punch down dough. Divide into 2 pieces. On lightly floured surface, roll or pat each piece into a 14″ x 7″ rectangle. Starting with the short end, tightly roll up the first piece. Pinch edges and ends to seal. Place in pan. Repeat. Cover and let rise in warm place until doubled.

5. Bake in oven preheated to 350 degrees for 45 minutes. Remove from pans and cool on wire racks. Serve or store.

Suggestions
This all-purpose bread makes delicious sandwiches, toast. bread crumbs and croutons.

NUTRITIONAL INFORMATION PER SERVING:

Serving size: 1 slice

Calories	90
Fat	18%
Carbohydrates	69%
Protein	3 gm
Sodium	70 mg
Calcium	6 mg
Iron	1 mg
Dietary fiber	3 gm
Cholesterol	0 mg

EXCHANGES:

Starch/Bread	1
Fat	½

M **Prep Time:** 20 min.
                (plus rising)
C **Cook Time:** 25-30 min.
S **Servings:**   30 slices
   Yield: 2 loaves

CRUSTY CONTINENTAL BREAD

See Also Pizza (page 109)

4-5 c. unbleached all-purpose flour
1 c. whole-wheat flour
2 pkgs. dry yeast
2 tsp. sugar
1¾ c. warm water (105-115 degrees)
⅓ c. vegetable oil
½ tsp. salt

Bread can be frozen, defrosted and reheated as a whole or partial loaf. After defrosting, wrap in foil and reheat at 400 degrees for 5 minutes or until just heated through. Do not dry out.

   1. Stir yeast and sugar into warm water (105 to 115 degrees) until dissolved. Set aside to proof.
   2. In extra-large mixing bowl, combine salt, whole-wheat flour and 2 c. white flour. Add proofed yeast mixture and oil, stirring until well blended. Gradually add 2 c. flour. Batter will be stiff and sticky.
   3. Turn mixture onto floured surface and sprinkle with ½ c. of remaining flour. Knead for 5 minutes, adding remaining flour if necessary. Dough should be sticky but not wet. Let rest for 5 minutes.
   4. Spray *2 10" x 15" baking sheets* with nonstick coating.
   5. Divide dough in half. Roll or pat each piece into an 8" x 12" rectangle. Starting with wide side, tightly roll up the first piece. Pinch edges together. Place on baking sheet seam side down. Repeat. Cover and let rise in a warm place until doubled. Approximately 1 hour.
   6. Bake in oven preheated to 375 degrees for 25 to 30 minutes. Cool on wire rack. Serve or store.

Suggestions
A good accompaniment to soups, stews and spaghetti. Ideal for garlic toast and French bread pizza.

NUTRITIONAL INFORMATION PER SERVING:

Serving size: 1 slice

Calories	98
Fat	22%
Carbohydrates	68%
Protein	3 gm
Sodium	33 mg
Calcium	5 mg
Iron	1 mg
Dietary fiber	1 gm
Cholesterol	0 mg

EXCHANGES:

Starch/Bread	1
Fat	½

| B | L | D | A/S | T |

Prep Time: 20 min.
    (plus rising)*
Cook Time: 3 min.
Servings: 30
Yield: (2) 10″ x 15″
    pizzas

PIZZA

*Crusty Continental Bread (page 108),
  taken to Step 4
*4½ c. Pizza Sauce (page 23)
  1 lb. part-skim mozzarella cheese, grated
  3 green, yellow and red bell peppers, diced
  8 oz. fresh mushrooms, sliced
  2 medium onions, sliced thin

Recipe freezes well. After baking, cool, cut into serving portions, wrap individually in foil and freeze. Reheat in foil (opened at top) or place servings on baking sheet and lay a piece of foil loosely over top. If reheated in microwave oven, crust will be less crisp.

1. Prepare Continental Bread through Step 4.
2. Begin Pizza Sauce or use defrosted sauce, warmed.
3. Divide dough in half. Lightly flour surface and roll or stretch dough to fit *2 10″ x 15″ nonstick baking sheets.* Cover and let rise in a warm spot until doubled in height. About 1 hour.
4. Meanwhile, grate cheese and steam vegetables.
5. Preheat oven to 400 degrees. Bake dough for 8 minutes. Remove from oven and top with desired amount of sauce (up to 2¼ c. per pizza), cheese and vegetables. Reduce heat to 350 degrees and bake for 18 to 20 minutes. Serve or store. Baking Pizza in 2 steps provides a crisp crust without overbaking the toppings.

Suggestions
Serve Pizza for any meal or snack. For a main meal, serve with a large tossed salad with dressing of choice or with Delightful Fruit Salad (page 39) and crisp vegetable sticks.

**NUTRITIONAL
INFORMATION
PER SERVING:**

Serving size: (1) 3″ x 3″
    piece

Calories	166
Fat	29%
Carbohydrates	53%
Protein	7 gm
Sodium	105 mg
Calcium	113 mg
Iron	1 mg
Dietary fiber	1 gm
Cholesterol	9 mg

EXCHANGES:

Starch/Bread	1
Poultry/Fish/Meat	½
Vegetable	⅕
Fat	1

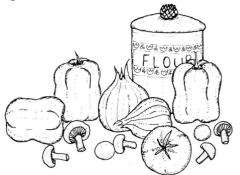

M **Prep Time:** 10 min.
C **Cook Time:** none
C **Servings:** 4
S **Yield:** 2-2¼ c.

TUNA OR SHRIMP SPREAD

TUNA SPREAD
6 ½-oz. can water-packed white tuna, drained
8-oz. can water chestnuts, drained and diced
3 tb. chopped green onion
¼ c. unsweetened crushed pineapple,
   well drained
½ tsp. lemon juice
1 tb. reduced-calorie and -fat mayonnaise
¼ c. nonfat yogurt
1 tsp. Mrs. Dash® lemon-and-herb seasoning
¼ tsp. curry powder

SHRIMP SPREAD
**Substitute 1 c. diced cooked shrimp (½ lb. raw)
for tuna and ½ tsp. dill for curry powder**

   1. In small bowl, flake tuna with fork to break into small pieces. If using shrimp, place in bowl.
   2. Add pineapple and onion. Mix together.
   3. In a *½ c. measuring cup,* blend yogurt, lemon juice, mayonnaise and seasonings. Add to tuna or shrimp and toss. Serve or store.

Suggestions
Use as a sandwich or cracker spread. Or divide recipe in half, placing 1 c. on lettuce; serve as a main dish salad.

**NUTRITIONAL
INFORMATION
PER SERVING:**

Tuna Spread

Serving size: ½ c.

Calories	124
Fat	15%
Carbohydrates	39%
Protein	15 gm
Sodium	185 mg
Calcium	38 mg
Iron	1 mg
Dietary fiber	0 gm
Cholesterol	18 mg

EXCHANGES:

Poultry/Fish/Meat	1½
Vegetable	½
Fat	½

Shrimp Spread

Serving size: ½ c.

Calories	103
Fat	13%
Carbohydrates	49%
Protein	10 gm
Sodium	77 mg
Calcium	62 mg
Iron	1 mg
Dietary fiber	0 gm
Cholesterol	62 mg

EXCHANGES:

Poultry/Fish/Meat	1
Vegetable	½
Fat	½

B L D A/S T

CHICKEN SPREAD

*2 c. diced cooked chicken
3 tb. chopped green onion
¼ c. chopped fresh parsley
¾ c. finely chopped celery
6 tb. nonfat yogurt
1 tb. reduced-fat and -calorie mayonnaise
2-3 tsp. Dijon-style mustard
Freshly ground pepper, to taste
Several broken walnuts, if desired

1. In medium bowl, combine chicken, celery, onion and parsley.
2. In ½ c. measuring cup, blend remaining ingredients. Add to chicken and blend. Serve or store.

Suggestions
Use as a sandwich or cracker spread. Or divide recipe in half, placing 1½ c. on lettuce, and serve as a main dish salad. Serve with whole-grain rolls.

NUTRITIONAL INFORMATION PER SERVING:

Serving size: ½ c.

Calories	81
Fat	25%
Carbohydrates	9%
Protein	13 gm
Sodium	71 mg
Calcium	42 mg
Iron	1 mg
Dietary fiber	0 gm
Cholesterol	33 mg

EXCHANGES:

Poultry/Fish/Meat	1½
Milk	Tr

B L D A/S T

CHICKEN SANDWICHES

*8 slices Healthy Bread Your Family Will Love (page 107)
*3 servings Breaded Chicken Breasts (page 78)
4 slices mild red onion
2 tb. Dijon-style mustard
1 tb. reduced-fat and -calorie mayonnaise
Fresh spinach or romaine lettuce, washed and dried

1. No mystery here; just assemble and eat or pack for a traveling meal.

NUTRITIONAL INFORMATION PER SERVING:

Serving size: 1 sandwich

Calories	358
Fat	25%
Carbohydrates	49%
Protein	23 gm
Sodium	421 mg
Calcium	105 mg
Iron	3 mg
Dietary fiber	3 gm
Cholesterol	39 mg

EXCHANGES:

Starch/Bread	2½
Poultry/Fish/Meat	1½
Vegetable	½
Fat	1

NO-YOLK EGG SALAD

NUTRITIONAL
INFORMATION
PER SERVING:

Serving size: 1/3 c.

Calories	47
Fat	18%
Carbohydrates	24%
Protein	7 gm
Sodium	129 mg
Calcium	41 mg
Iron	0 mg
Dietary fiber	0 gm
Cholesterol	1 mg

*10 hard-boiled egg whites, finely chopped
2 oz. jar chopped pimento, drained and
**   patted dry**
3 tb. finely chopped red or green onion
1 tb. reduced-calorie and -fat mayonnaise
1 tb. Dijon-style mustard
6 tb. nonfat yogurt
2 tsp. parsley
Freshly ground pepper, to taste

Recipe will keep for several days covered in the
refrigerator. Mix again before using.

1. In small bowl or covered refrigerator container,
mix mayonnaise, mustard, yogurt, and parsley until
well-blended.
2. Blend in egg whites, pimento and onion. Add
pepper, if desired.

EXCHANGES:

Poultry/Fish/Meat	1/2
Fat	1/5

Suggestions
Use as a sandwich or cracker spread.

Clockwise from top: Delicious Milkshakes (strawberry-orange), Pineapple Dessert, Raspberry Delight.

INDEX

Delicious Milkshakes (7 versions)   116
Raspberry Delight   120
Pineapple Dessert   121
Smooth Apple Dessert   122
Baked Fruit Dessert   123
Fruit Cookies   124
Fruit Bars   125
Your-Choice Coffee Cake   126

DESSERTS AND BEVERAGES

Now you can have your cake and eat it, too. Your-Choice Coffee Cake, that is.

These desserts are low in calories, but not in flavor. All recipes call for skim milk and little or no fat. Their flavor comes from fruit: fresh, frozen, canned, concentrated or conserved.

They are ideal for snacks, or even as light meals. For instance, try a Delicious Milkshake as a ''sports meal,'' a fast breakfast or an afternoon snack.

Hints

- Keep a can of orange juice concentrate in the freezer for use in dessert recipes.
- Peel ripe (not mushy) bananas and slice into rounds. Wrap in foil and freeze. Take directly from freezer and add banana slices to milkshakes.
- Top fresh fruit with a dab of non-fat yogurt or Fruit Dressing for a light dessert with pizzazz.

Select a beverage

Choose one item from each column. Place fruit juice and mineral water in a glass. Stir and add ice and fruit. Or, combine several servings of mineral water and juice in a pitcher and pour over fruit and ice in individual glasses.

Mineral water

(unsalted)
Plain
Orange
Berry
Lemon
Lime

Fruit garnish

Firm strawberries
Orange slice
Lime slice
Lemon slice

Unsweetened fruit juice

¼ c. fresh or frozen or 1 tb. frozen concentrate

Orange
Pineapple
Raspberry
Grape

M   **Prep Time:** 1-2 min.
C   **Cook Time:** none
    Servings: 1
S

DELICIOUS MILKSHAKES

BLUEBERRY SHAKE

½ c. nonfat yogurt
1 c. skim milk
½ large, ripe fresh or frozen banana
1 tb. blueberry conserve
½ c. fresh or frozen unsweetened blueberries
2 ice cubes

BANANA-ORANGE SHAKE

1½ c. skim milk
½ large, ripe, fresh or frozen banana
2 tb. frozen orange juice concentrate
2 ice cubes

Recipe can be doubled. Prepare all variations using this method.

1. Combine all ingredients in blender. Blend on high for 30 to 45 seconds or until smooth. Serve immediately.

Suggestions

There's no excuse for skipping breakfast when you can make this nutritious milkshake in 2 minutes. Have one for breakfast, along with a muffin. It also makes a good dessert for those weaning themselves from ice cream.

Try one of the following variations , or use your imagination to create your own.

**NUTRITIONAL
INFORMATION
PER SERVING:**

Blueberry Shake

Calories	285
Fat	5%
Carbohydrates	72%
Protein	16 gm
Sodium	214 mg
Calcium	538 mg
Iron	1 mg
Dietary fiber	4 gm
Cholesterol	6 mg

EXCHANGES:

Fruit	2
Milk	2

Banana-Orange Shake

Calories	229
Fat	4%
Carbohydrates	73%
Protein	14 gm
Sodium	191 mg
Calcium	466 mg
Iron	0 mg
Dietary fiber	2 gm
Cholesterol	6 mg

EXCHANGES:

Fruit	1½
Milk	1½

M   **Prep Time:** 1-2 min.
C   **Cook Time:** none
    Servings: 1
S

DELICIOUS MILKSHAKES
Continued

ORANGE SHAKE
1½ c. skim milk
3 tb. frozen orange juice concentrate
2 ice cubes

RASPBERRY SHAKE
1½ c. skim milk
½ large, ripe, fresh or frozen banana
½ c. fresh or frozen unsweetened raspberries
1 tb. raspberry conserve
2 ice cubes

Recipe can be doubled. Prepare all variations using this method.

1. Combine all ingredients in blender. Blend on high for 30 to 45 seconds or until smooth. Serve immediately.

NUTRITIONAL INFORMATION PER SERVING:

Orange Shake

Calories	197
Fat	3%
Carbohydrates	69%
Protein	14 gm
Sodium	190 mg
Calcium	466 mg
Iron	0 mg
Dietary fiber	0 gm
Cholesterol	6 mg

EXCHANGES:

Fruit	1¼
Milk	1½

Raspberry Shake

Calories	256
Fat	5%
Carbohydrates	72%
Protein	14 gm
Sodium	190 mg
Calcium	470 mg
Iron	1 mg
Dietary fiber	4 gm
Cholesterol	6 mg

EXCHANGES:

Fruit	2
Milk	1½

M
C **Prep Time:** 1-2 min.
S **Cook Time:** none
Servings: 1

DELICIOUS MILKSHAKES
Continued

STRAWBERRY-ORANGE SHAKE

1½ c. skim milk
½ large, ripe, fresh or frozen banana
½ c. fresh or frozen unsweetened strawberries
1 tb. frozen orange juice concentrate
1 tb. strawberry conserve
2 ice cubes

BANANA-PINEAPPLE SHAKE

1½ c. skim milk
½ large, ripe, fresh or frozen banana
½ c. canned, unsweetened crushed pineapple
    and juice
2 ice cubes

Recipe can be doubled. Prepare all variations using
this method.

1. Combine all ingredients in blender. Blend on high
for 30 to 45 seconds or until smooth. Serve
immediately.

**NUTRITIONAL
INFORMATION
PER SERVING:**

**Strawberry-Orange
Shake**

Calories	274
Fat	4%
Carbohydrates	75%
Protein	14 gm
Sodium	192 mg
Calcium	473 mg
Iron	1 mg
Dietary fiber	3 gm
Cholesterol	6 mg

EXCHANGES:

Fruit	2½
Milk	1½

**Banana-Pineapple
Shake**

Calories	222
Fat	5%
Carbohydrates	72%
Protein	13 gm
Sodium	190 mg
Calcium	462 mg
Iron	1 mg
Dietary fiber	3 gm
Cholesterol	6 mg

EXCHANGES:

Fruit	1½
Milk	1½

M

C

S

Prep Time: 1-2 min.
Cook Time: none
Servings: 1

DELICIOUS MILKSHAKES
Continued

STRAWBERRY SHAKE
1½ c. skim milk
1 c. fresh or frozen unsweetened strawberries
1 tb. strawberry conserve
2 ice cubes

Recipe can be doubled. Prepare all variations using this method.

1. Combine all ingredients in blender. Blend on high for 30 to 45 seconds or until smooth. Serve immediately.

**NUTRITIONAL
INFORMATION
PER SERVING:**

Strawberry Shake

Calories	223
Fat	4%
Carbohydrates	70%
Protein	13 gm
Sodium	192 mg
Calcium	476 mg
Iron	1 mg
Dietary fiber	4 gm
Cholesterol	6 mg

EXCHANGES:

Fruit	1½
Milk	1½

Desserts and Beverages 119

B L D | A/S | T

M **Prep Time:** 5 min.
C **Cook Time:** 5 min.
   (Then chill)
| S | **Servings:** 8
   Yield: 4 c.

RASPBERRY DELIGHT

3 c. skim milk
4 tb. cornstarch
¼ c. frozen orange juice concentrate
¼ c. raspberry conserve
2 c. unsweetened fresh or frozen raspberries
8 whole raspberries and 16 sliced almonds,
if desired

Recipe can be made in advance.
When using frozen raspberries, break apart while they are still in the bag.

1. Whisk together milk and cornstarch until well-blended.
2. In cup, mix raspberry conserve and orange concentrate with fork until smooth. Set aside.
3. In *2-qt. sauce pot,* cook milk and cornstarch over medium-high heat, stirring constantly, until thick and bubbly. Cook and stir 1 minute longer. Remove from heat.
4. Add conserve mixture and raspberries. Stir until well-blended and raspberries are evenly distributed.
5. Pour into stemmed glasses. Let cool. Garnish with whole raspberries and sliced almonds, if desired. Cover and refrigerate.

NUTRITIONAL INFORMATION PER SERVING:

Serving size: ½ c.

Calories	94
Fat	4%
Carbohydrates	79%
Protein	4 gm
Sodium	48 mg
Calcium	122 mg
Iron	0 mg
Dietary fiber	2 gm
Cholesterol	2 mg

EXCHANGES:

Fruit	1
Milk	½

B L D A/S T

M **Prep Time:** 5 min.
   Cook Time: 5 min.
C   (Then chill)
S **Servings:** 8
   Yield: 5⅓ c.

PINEAPPLE DESSERT

**2 20-oz. cans unsweetened crushed pineapple,
    well drained (reserve liquid for another
    recipe)**
2 c. skim milk
3 tb. cornstarch
1 tsp. vanilla
½ c. golden raisins
**Sliced strawberries, blueberries or 2 tb. ground
walnuts, if desired**

Recipe can be prepared in advance.

1. In *3-qt. saucepot,* whisk together milk and cornstarch until well-blended. Cook over medium-high heat,
stirring constantly until mixture is thick and bubbly.
Cook and stir 1 minute longer. Remove from heat. Add
raisins and vanilla. Stir to blend and soften raisins.

2. Meanwhile, puree 1 can of pineapple in food
processor or blender. Add remaining pineapple and
pineapple puree to milk mixture. Blend. Spoon into
stemmed dessert glasses. Cool.

3. If desired, garnish with sliced strawberries, whole
blueberries or ground walnuts. Cover and refrigerate.

Suggestions
Serve with whole-grain crackers and 8 ounces of nonfat yogurt for lunch.

**NUTRITIONAL
INFORMATION
PER SERVING:**

Serving size: ⅔ c.

Calories	95
Fat	4%
Carbohydrates	86%
Protein	3 gm
Sodium	33 mg
Calcium	85 mg
Iron	0 mg
Dietary fiber	2 gm
Cholesterol	1 mg

EXCHANGES:

Fruit	1
Milk	½

SMOOTH APPLE DESSERT

2½ lbs. cooking apples
½ c. orange juice
¼ c. golden raisins
1½ tsp. cinnamon
1 c. skim milk
3 tb. cornstarch
2 tb. finely ground walnuts, if desired

Will keep covered in refrigerator for several days.
Can be reheated.

1. Wash, peel, core and thinly slice apples.
Combine in *3-qt. sauce pot,* apples with orange juice
and raisins.
2. Cover and cook over medium heat until apples
are soft (about 20 minutes). Remove from heat. In food
processor, combine apples and cinnamon. Puree until
smooth, scraping sides often.
3. While apples are in food processor, whisk
together milk and cornstarch until well-blended, using
the same 3-qt. pot. Cook over medium-high heat, stirring constantly, until thick and bubbly. Cook and stir 1
minute longer. Add to food processor and puree all
ingredients together until smooth and well-blended.
4. Pour into small serving bowls. Garnish with
walnuts, if desired. Serve warm or cool. Cover and
refrigerate.

Suggestions
Serve warm as a sauce over another dessert. Makes
a light breakfast or lunch when served with Oat-Bran
Muffins (page 101).

**NUTRITIONAL
INFORMATION
PER SERVING:**

Serving size: ½ c.

Calories	91
Fat	3%
Carbohydrates	91%
Protein	2 gm
Sodium	17 mg
Calcium	53 mg
Iron	0 mg
Dietary fiber	3 gm
Cholesterol	0 mg

EXCHANGES:

Fruit	1½
Milk	Tr

B L D A/S T

M **Prep Time:** 15 min.
C **Cook Time:** 45-60 min.
   Servings: 12
S **Yield:** 6 c.

BAKED FRUIT DESSERT

2½ lbs. cooking apples, washed, cored and
    thinly sliced
12 dried apricots, thinly sliced
¼ c. chopped walnuts
1 16-oz. can unsweetened sliced peaches,
    drained
2 tb. quick-cooking tapioca
2 tb. nonfat yogurt
2 tb. peach or orange conserve
2 tb. frozen orange juice concentrate
1 tsp. cinnamon

Recipe can be assembled in advance, covered and
refrigerated.
    1. In large bowl, combine sliced apples, apricots,
peaches and walnuts. Sprinkle with tapioca.
    2. In small container, mix remaining ingredients until
smooth. Pour over fruit. Toss to coat.
    3. Preheat oven to 400 degrees. Spray *9″ x 13″*
nonstick baking pan with nonstick coating.
    4. Place fruit mixture in pan, cover with foil and bake
for 45 to 60 minutes or until apples are soft. Stir and
serve warm or cold.

Suggestions
Serve for dessert or with nonfat yogurt for breakfast.

**NUTRITIONAL
INFORMATION
PER SERVING:**

Serving size: ½ c.

Calories	109
Fat	15%
Carbohydrates	81%
Protein	1 gm
Sodium	5 mg
Calcium	18 mg
Iron	1 mg
Dietary fiber	3 gm
Cholesterol	0 mg

EXCHANGES:

Fruit	1½
Fat	½

B ☐L☐ D A/S ☐T☐

M   **Prep Time:** 15 min.
☐C☐ **Cook Time:** 8 min.
    Servings: 30
S   **Yield:**   30

FRUIT COOKIES
Raspberry Or Blueberry

½ c. unbleached all-purpose flour
1½ c. old-fashioned oats
½ tsp. baking soda
1 c. crunchy wheat-and-barley cereal
6 tb. raspberry conserve
3 tb. vegetable oil
1 tsp. vanilla
¼ c. ½%-fat buttermilk
2 egg whites
2 tb. grated orange rind
1 c. frozen unsweetened raspberries
    OR 1 c. frozen unsweetened blueberries

Recipe can be doubled. Freezes well.

1. In small bowl, mix first four ingredients. Set aside.
2. In larger mixing bowl, mix well all remaining ingredients except frozen fruit with electric beaters. Add dry ingredients and blend again.
3. Gently fold in fruit with wooden spoon until it is evenly distributed.
4. Preheat oven to 375 degrees. Spray *two 10″ x 15″ baking sheets* with nonstick coating.
5. Drop cookie dough by rounded teaspoonfuls onto baking sheets.
6. Bake for 8 minutes, remove from baking sheet. Cool on wire racks (fruit may stain other surfaces). Store in airtight container for up to 3 days. Freeze if longer storage time is needed and remove a few hours before serving.

Note: Prepare both kinds of cookies by dividing batter in half after Step 2. Add ½ c. blueberries to one half and ½ c. raspberries to the other. Or double ingredients and add 1 c. of each fruit, using the same method.

Suggestions
This good-for-you cookie packs easily for lunch and travels well. Pack directly from freezer, if desired.

NUTRITIONAL INFORMATION PER SERVING:

Serving size: 1 cookie

Calories	61
Fat	27%
Carbohydrates	62%
Protein	2 gm
Sodium	38 mg
Calcium	8 mg
Iron	0 mg
Dietary fiber	2 gm
Cholesterol	0 mg

EXCHANGES:

Starch/Bread	½
Fruit	Tr
Fat	⅓

B   L   D   A/S   T

M
C   **Prep Time:** 15 min.
    Cook Time: 18 min.
    Servings: 20
S   **Yield:** (1) 9" x 13" pan

FRUIT BARS

1½ c. unbleached all-purpose flour
½ c. whole-wheat flour
¼ tsp. baking soda
½ tsp. cinnamon
3 tb. vegetable oil
2 egg whites
1 tsp. almond extract
⅓ c. skim milk
1¼ c. golden raisins, chopped
¼ c. unsweetened pineapple, well drained
6 tb. pineapple or peach conserve
2 tb. conserve, if desired

Recipe can be doubled. Freezes well for do-ahead baking.

1. In medium bowl, mix flours, soda, and cinnamon. Set aside.

2. In mixing bowl, mix well egg whites, oil, almond extract and milk with electric mixer. Stir in pineapple, raisins and conserve. Add flour mixture to moist ingredients, mixing until just blended. Do not overbeat.

3. Preheat oven to 350 degrees. Spray *9" x 13" nonstick pan* with nonstick coating.

4. Spread batter evenly in pan and bake for 18 minutes.

5. Remove from oven. If desired, warm 2 tb. conserve and use as a glaze. Let cool. Cut into 2" x 2½" bars and store in airtight container.

**NUTRITIONAL
INFORMATION
PER SERVING:**

Serving size: 2" x 2½"
               bar

Calories	103
Fat	20%
Carbohydrates	71%
Protein	2 gm
Sodium	19 mg
Calcium	13 mg
Iron	1 mg
Dietary fiber	1 gm
Cholesterol	0 mg

EXCHANGES:

Starch/Bread	½
Fruit	½
Fat	½

M **Prep Time:** 15 min.
C **Cook Time:** 15 min.
Servings: 12
S **Yield:** (1) 9" x 13" pan

YOUR-CHOICE COFFEE CAKE
Date-Apricot, Blueberry, Raisin

½ c. oat bran
1½ c. unbleached all-purpose flour
2½ tsp. baking powder
¾ c. ½%-fat buttermilk
¼ c. orange marmalade conserve
¼ c. frozen orange juice concentrate
2 tb. grated orange rind
2 tb. vegetable oil
1 egg white
2 tb. conserve, if desired

DATE-APRICOT
⅓ c. chopped dates
⅓ c. chopped apricots

BLUEBERRY
¾ c. fresh or frozen blueberries
Add 1 tb. conserve

RAISIN
⅔ c. golden raisins, chopped

Freezes well when cut into individual portions. Freeze if cake will not be served within 2 days.

1. In medium bowl, combine dry ingredients and fruit (except blueberries, which should be folded in last).
2. In *2 c. measuring cup,* combine milk and remaining ingredients. Mix with fork until well-blended.
3. Preheat oven to 400 degrees, spray *9" x 13" baking pan* with nonstick coating.
4. Add moist ingredients to dry ingredients and blend well. If using blueberries, fold in until they are evenly distributed.
5. Bake for 13 to 15 minutes. Test with toothpick after 13 minutes. Remove from oven. If desired, heat 2 tb. conserve and glaze cake top. Serve or store.

NUTRITIONAL INFORMATION PER SERVING:

Serving size: 3" x 3¼" portion

Calories	158
Fat	20%
Carbohydrates	69%
Protein	4 gm
Sodium	92 mg
Calcium	42 mg
Iron	1 mg
Dietary fiber	1 gm
Cholesterol	1 mg

EXCHANGES:

Starch/Bread	1
Fruit	½
Fat	1

Week 1, Day 2: Dinner. *Clockwise from bottom: Meatless Chili, whole-grain bread, tossed salad with Vinaigrette, fresh fruit.*

The Four-Week Menu Plan provides 28 days of balanced diets featuring recipes from this book. It is intended to offer a starting point for those who would like to add structure to their daily eating patterns.

A few quick notes about the plan.

- Meatless days are highlighted.
- Fruits, vegetables, whole grains and dairy products are included each day.
- Calories and other nutrients have been distributed throughout each day's menu.

The menu plan is calculated at four daily caloric levels: 1,200, 1,500, 1,800 and 2,100 (as in all recipes, caloric values are good approximations rather than exact values). To determine the appropriate quantity of food, locate the column containing your chosen caloric level. Move down to the specific recipe and multiply the number in the column by the serving size listed for that entry. (If you are preparing meals for others, multiply that quantity by the number of people eating.) That will tell you how many servings of the recipe you'll need to prepare.

You can use the plan as written for up to four weeks. Increase or decrease time span according to your needs.

Planning is an important part of following any menu plan. Shopping is another. Having the necessary ingredients available makes it easier to follow recipes closely—giving you a better chance of sticking to your plan.

Always prepare a shopping list before grocery shopping. And remember: Never shop on an empty stomach!

WEEK 1 DAY 1

RECIPE SERVING SIZE		TOTAL DAILY CALORIES (Number of Servings)			
		1200	1500	1800	2100
B	Oats & Fruit Breakfast (page 102), 1 c.	1	1	1½	2
	Healthy Bread Your Family Will Love (page 107), 1 slice	1	2	2	2
L	Pita Pockets With Tomatoes (page 71), ½ pocket	1	2	2	2
	Banana-Pineapple Milkshake (page 118) 1	1	1	1	1
D	Marinated Chicken Stir-Fry (page 83), 1¾ c.	1	1½	2	2½
	Basic Rice (page 67), ⅓ c.	2	3	3	3½
A/S	Popcorn, 3 c.	½	½	1	1

WEEK 1 DAY 2 MEATLESS Meals

RECIPE SERVING SIZE		TOTAL DAILY CALORIES (Number of Servings)			
		1200	1500	1800	2100
B	Strawberry-Banana Salad (page 40), ⅔ c.	1	1	1	2
	Nonfat Plain Yogurt or Skim Milk, 8 oz.	½	1	1	1
	Healthy Bread Your Family Will Love (page 107), 1 slice	1	2	2	2
	Margarine, 1 tsp.	1	1	1	1
L	All-Around Potato (page 51), 1 potato	1	1	1½	1½
	Marinated Vegetables (page 56), ¾ c.	½	1	1	1
	Skim Milk, 8 oz.	1	1	1	1
D	Meatless Chili (page 19), 1½ c.	1	1	1½	2
	Whole-Grain Bread, 1 slice	1	1	2	2
	Tossed Salad, 2 c.	½	1	1	1
	Vinaigrette (page 42), 1 tb.	1	1	2	2
A/S	Fresh Fruit, 1	1	1	1	2

WEEK 1 DAY 3

TOTAL DAILY CALORIES
(Number of Servings)

RECIPE SERVING SIZE	1200	1500	1800	2100
B Plain Pancakes (page 104), 2	1	1	2	2
Fresh Fruit, 1				
or Fruit Juice, ½ c.	1	2	2	2
Skim Milk or Nonfat Plain Yogurt, 8 oz.	1	1	1	1
L Meatless Chili (page 19), 1½ c.	1	1	1	1½
Bread Sticks, 2	1	2	2	2
Fresh Fruit, 1	1	2	2	2
Skim Milk, 8 oz.	1	1	1	1
Margarine, 1 tsp.	1	1	2	2
D Tuna or Salmon Toasts (page 91), 2 slices	1	1	1	1½
Marinated Vegetables (page 56), ¾ c.	1	1	2	2
Fresh Fruit, 1	1	2	2	2
A/S Fruit Cookie (page 124), 1	1	1	1	2

WEEK 1 DAY 4 MEATLESS Meals

TOTAL DAILY CALORIES
(Number of Servings)

RECIPE SERVING SIZE	1200	1500	1800	2100
B Cornmeal-Bean Squares (page 69), 1 piece	1	1	2	2
Fresh Fruit, 1 or				
Fruit Juice, ½ c.	1	2	2	2
Skim Milk or Nonfat Plain Yogurt, 8 oz.	1	1	1	1
L Twice-Baked Potato (page 62), 1 potato	1	1	1	1½
Skim Milk, 8 oz.	1	1	1	1
Delightful Fruit Salad (page 39), 1 c.	½	1	1	1
D Pizza (page 109), 1 slice	2	3	3	4
Tossed Salad, 2 c.	½	1	1	1
Vinaigrette (page 42), 1 tb.	1	1	2	2
A/S Popcorn, 3 c.	½	1	1	1

WEEK 1 DAY 5   M̲E̲A̲T̲L̲E̲S̲S̲ *Meals*

TOTAL DAILY CALORIES
(Number of Servings)

RECIPE SERVING SIZE	1200	1500	1800	2100
B Banana Bread (page 100), 1 slice	1	2	2	3
Skim Milk or Nonfat Plain Yogurt, 8 oz.	1	1	1	1
Fresh Fruit, 1 or				
Fruit Juice, ½ c.	1	1	2	2
L Salad That's A Meal (page 30), 4 c.	1	1	1	1½
Yogurt-Poppyseed Dressing,				
(page 43), 2 tb.	1	1	2	2
Skim Milk, 8 oz.	1	1	1	1
Whole-Grain Roll, 1	1	2	2	2
D Cabbage-Potato Soup (page 10),				
1½ c.	1	1½	1½	1½
Oat Bran Muffin (page 101), 1	1	1	1½	2
Margarine, 1 tsp.	1	1	1	1
Pear-Gelatin Salad (page 41), ¾ c.	1	1	1	1
A/S Fresh Fruit, 1	1	1	1	1

WEEK 1 DAY 6

TOTAL DAILY CALORIES
(Number of Servings)

RECIPE SERVING SIZE	1200	1500	1800	2100
B Cornmeal-Bean Squares (page 69),				
1 piece	1	1	2	2
Fresh Fruit, 1 or				
Fruit Juice, ½ c.	1	2	2	2
Skim Milk or Nonfat Plain Yogurt, 8 oz.	1	1	1	1
L Pizza (page 109), 1 slice	2	3	3	4
Tossed Salad, 2 c.	1	2	2	2
Vinaigrette (page 42), 1 tb.	1	1	2	2
Fresh Fruit, 1	1	1	2	2
D Scallop Stir-Fry (page 90), 1 c.	1	1½	1½	2
Basic Rice (page 67), ⅓ c.	3	3	3	4
A/S Fresh Fruit, 1	1	1	1	2

MEATLESS
Meals

TOTAL DAILY CALORIES
(Number of Servings)

RECIPE SERVING SIZE	1200	1500	1800	2100
B All-Around Potato (page 51), 1 potato	1	1	1	1½
Fresh Fruit, 1 or				
Fruit Juice, ½ c.	1	1	2	2
L Cabbage and Potato Soup (page 10),				
1½ c.	1	1½	2	2
Skim Milk or Nonfat Plain Yogurt, 8 oz.	1	1	1	1
Fresh Fruit, 1	1	1	2	2
D Spaghetti Sauce With Tofu (page 21),				
1 c.	1	1½	2	2
Pasta, ½ c.	2	2	2½	3
Marinated Vegetables (page 56), ¾ c.	1	1	1	1
Crusty Continental Bread (page 108),				
1 slice	1	2	2	3
A/S Raspberry Delight (page 120), ½ c.	1	1	1	1

WEEK 2 DAY 1

RECIPE SERVING SIZE	TOTAL DAILY CALORIES (Number of Servings)			
	1200	1500	1800	2100
B Unconventional French Toast (page 105), 2 slices	1	1	1	2
Fresh Fruit, 1 or				
Fruit Juice, ½ c.	1	1	2	2
Skim Milk or Nonfat Plain Yogurt, 8 oz.	1	1	1	1
L Spaghetti Sauce With Tofu (page 21), ½ c.	1	1½	1½	1½
Pasta, ½ c.	2	2	2½	2½
Bread Sticks, 2	1	2	2	2
D McHealthy Chicken Nuggets (page 85), 6	1	1	1½	2
Potato Salad With Egg (page 31), 1¼ c.	1	1½	1½	2
A/S Pineapple Dessert (page 121), ⅔ c.	1	1	1	1

WEEK 2 DAY 2 MEATLESS Meals

RECIPE SERVING SIZE	TOTAL DAILY CALORIES (Number of Servings)			
	1200	1500	1800	2100
B Healthy Bread Your Family Will Love (page 107), 1 slice	2	2	2	2½
Healthy Topping (page 26), 1 tb.	2	2	2	2
Fresh Fruit, 1	1	2	2	2
Skim Milk or Nonfat Plain Yogurt, 8 oz.	1	1	1	1
L Potato Salad With Egg (page 31), 1¼ c.	1½	1½	2	2½
Vegetable Sticks, ½ c.	2	2	2	2
Skim Milk or Nonfat Plain Yogurt, 8 oz.	1	1	1	1
D Surprise Quiche (page 63), 1 slice	2	2½	3	3½
Delightful Fruit Salad (page 39), 1 c.	1	1½	2	2½
Whole-Grain Roll, 1	1	1	2	2
A/S Popcorn, 3 c.	1	1	1	1

WEEK 2 DAY 3 Meatless *Meals*

TOTAL DAILY CALORIES
(Number of Servings)

RECIPE SERVING SIZE	1200	1500	1800	2100
B Surprise Quiche (page 63), 1 slice	1	2	2½	3
Skim Milk or Nonfat Plain Yogurt, 8 oz.	1	1	1	1
Fresh Fruit, 1 or				
Fruit Juice, ½ c.	2	2	2	2
L Delightful Fruit Salad (page 39), 1 c.	1	1½	2	2½
Oat Bran Muffin (page 101), 1	1	1	2	2
Skim Milk or Nonfat Plain Yogurt, 8 oz.	1	1	1	1
D Cream of Asparagus Soup (page 8), 1¼ c.	1	1½	2	2½
Cold Bean Salad (page 36), ½ c.	1	1	1	1½
Crusty Continental Bread (page 108), 1 slice	2	2	2	3
A/S Baked Fruit Dessert (page 123), ½ c.	1	1	1	1

WEEK 2 DAY 4

TOTAL DAILY CALORIES
(Number of Servings)

RECIPE SERVING SIZE	1200	1500	1800	2100
B Pancakes With Blueberries (page 104), 2	2	2	2½	3
Skim Milk or Nonfat Plain Yogurt, 8 oz.	1	1	1	1
L Cream of Asparagus Soup (page 8), 1¼ c.	1	1½	2	2½
Bread Sticks, 2	2	2	2½	3
Margarine, 1 tsp.	1	1	2	2
Fresh Fruit, 1	2	2	2	2
D Oven-Baked Chicken With Tomato Sauce (page 79), 1 piece	1	1½	1½	1½
Fancy Steamed Vegetables (page 55), ½ c.	2	2	2	2
Great Boiled Potatoes (page 50), ⅔ c.	1	1½	2	2½
A/S Raspberry Delight (page 120), ½ c.	1	1	1	1

WEEK 2 DAY 5 ***MEATLESS Meals***

TOTAL DAILY CALORIES
(Number of Servings)

RECIPE SERVING SIZE	1200	1500	1800	2100
B Wheat & Fruit Breakfast (page 103),				
1⅓ c.	1	1	1½	2
Whole-Wheat Bread, 1 slice	1	2	2	2
Margarine, 1 tsp.	1	2	2	2
L Chilled Orange-Rice Salad (page 38),				
1 c.	1	1	2	2½
Skim Milk or Nonfat Plain Yogurt, 8 oz.	1	1	1	1
Whole-Wheat Roll, 1	1	1	1	1
D Healthy Burritos (page 70), 1	1	1½	1½	1½
Fresh Fruit, 1	1	1	1	1
Steamed Vegetables of Choice, ½ c.	2	2	3	3
A/S Popcorn, 3 c.	½	1	1	1

WEEK 2 DAY 6 ***MEATLESS Meals***

TOTAL DAILY CALORIES
(Number of Servings)

RECIPE SERVING SIZE	1200	1500	1800	2100
B Healthy Bread Your Family Will Love				
(page 107), 1 slice	2	2	2	2½
Healthy Topping (page 26), 1 tb.	2	2	2	2
Skim Milk or Nonfat Plain Yogurt, 8 oz.	1	1	1	1
Fresh Fruit, 1	2	2	2	3
L Salad That's A Meal (page 30), 4 c.	1	1	1½	1½
Yogurt-Dijon Dressing (page 43), 2 tb.	1	1	2	2
Skim Milk or Nonfat Plain Yogurt, 8 oz.	1	1	1	1
Whole-Grain Roll, 1	1	2	2	3
D Cornmeal-Bean Squares (page 69),				
1 piece	1	1½	2	2½
Fancy Steamed Vegetables				
(page 55), ½ c.	2	2	2	2
Pineapple Dessert (page 121), ⅔ c.	1	1	1	1½
A/S Popcorn, 3 c.	1	1	1½	1½

TOTAL DAILY CALORIES
(Number of Servings)

RECIPE SERVING SIZE	1200	1500	1800	2100
B Cornmeal-Bean Squares (page 69), 1 piece	1	1	2	2
Fresh Fruit, 1 or Fruit Juice, ½ c.	1	2	2	2
Skim Milk or Nonfat Plain Yogurt, 8 oz.	1	1	1	1
L Tuna or Shrimp Spread (page 110), ½ c.	1	1	1½	2
Healthy Bread Your Family Will Love (page 107), 1 slice	2	2	2½	3
Margarine, 1 tsp.	1	1	2	2
Skim Milk or Nonfat Plain Yogurt, 8 oz.	1	1	1	1
D Thick And Hearty Bean-Barley Soup (page 14), 2 c.	1	1½	1½	2
Whole-Grain Roll, 1	1	2	2	2
Margarine, 1 tsp.	1	2	2	2
A/S Fresh Fruit, 1	1	1	1	1

WEEK 3 DAY 1

RECIPE SERVING SIZE	1200	1500	1800	2100
B All-Around Potato (page 51), 1 potato	1	1	1	1
Fresh Fruit, 1 or				
Fruit Juice, ½ c.	1	2	2	2
L Thick And Hearty Bean-Barley Soup				
(page 14), 2 c.	½	1	1½	2
Skim Milk, 8 oz.	1	1	1	1
Whole-Wheat Roll, 1	1	2	2	3
Margarine, 1 tsp.	1	1	2	2
D Suburban Chicken (page 84), 1	1	1	1	1
Basic Rice (page 67), ⅓ c.	2	3	4	5
A/S Fresh Fruit, 1	1	1	1	1

WEEK 3 DAY 2 MEATLESS *Meals*

RECIPE SERVING SIZE	1200	1500	1800	2100
B Strawberry-Orange Milkshake				
(page 118), 1	1	1	1½	1½
Oat Bran Muffin (page 101), 1	1	1	1	2
L Salad That's A Meal (page 30), 4 c.	1	1½	1½	1½
Vinaigrette Light (page 42), 1 tb.	2	2½	2½	2½
Fresh Fruit, 1	1	2	3	3
D Meatless Shepherd's Pie (page 61),				
⅛ recipe	1	1	1½	1½
Pear-Gelatin Salad (page 41), ¾ c.	1	2	2	2
A/S Popcorn, 3 c.	1	1	1	1

WEEK 3 DAY 3

TOTAL DAILY CALORIES
(Number of Servings)

RECIPE SERVING SIZE	1200	1500	1800	2100
B Pear-Gelatin Salad (page 41), ¾ c.	1	1½	1½	2
Oat Bran Muffin (page 101), 1	1	1	2	2
Skim Milk or Nonfat Plain Yogurt, 8 oz.	1	1	1	1
L Tuna or Shrimp Spread (page 110), ½ c.	1	1	1½	2
Healthy Bread Your Family Will Love (page 107), 1 slice	2	2	2½	3
Skim Milk, 8 oz.	1	1	1	1
D Stuffed Pasta Shells (page 65), 4	1	1½	1½	2
Fancy Steamed Vegetables (page 55), ½ c.	1	2	2	2
Healthy Bread Your Family Will Love (page 107), 1 slice	2	2	2½	3
A/S Smooth Apple Dessert (page 122), ½ c.	1	1	1	1½

WEEK 3 DAY 4

TOTAL DAILY CALORIES
(Number of Servings)

RECIPE SERVING SIZE	1200	1500	1800	2100
B Unconventional French Toast (page 105), 2 slices	1	1½	1½	2½
Fresh Fruit, 1 or Fruit Juice, ½ c.	2	2	2	3
Skim Milk or Nonfat Plain Yogurt, 8 oz.	1	1	1	1
L No-Yolk Egg Salad (page 112), ⅓ c.	2	2	2	2
Healthy Bread Your Family Will Love (page 107), 1 slice	2	3	3	3
Skim Milk, 8 oz.	1	1	1	1
D Salmon Filet With Dill Sauce (page 89), 4 oz.	1	1½	2	2
Great Boiled Potatoes (page 50), ⅔ c.	1½	2	2½	3
Marinated Vegetables (page 56), ¾ c.	1	1	1	1
A/S Popcorn, 3 c.	1	1	1	1

WEEK 3 DAY 5 MEATLESS Meals

RECIPE SERVING SIZE	TOTAL DAILY CALORIES (Number of Servings)			
	1200	1500	1800	2100
B Banana-Pineapple Milkshake (page 118), 1	1	1	1½	1½
Oat Bran Muffin (page 101), 1	1	1	1	2
L Hot or Cold Vegetable Soup (page 16), 1½ c.	1	1	1	1½
Crusty Continental Bread (page 108), 1 slice	1	2	2½	3
Margarine, 1 tsp.	1	1	1	1
D Hot Pasta Salad With Beans (page 33), 1¼ c.	1	1¼	1½	1½
Delightful Fruit Salad (page 39), 1 c.	½	1	1	1
A/S Healthy Bread Your Family Will Love (page 107), 1 slice	½	1	1	1
Healthy Topping (page 26), 1 tb.	½	1	1	1

WEEK 3 DAY 6

RECIPE SERVING SIZE	TOTAL DAILY CALORIES (Number of Servings)			
	1200	1500	1800	2100
B All-Around Potato (page 51), 1 potato	1	1	1	1½
Fresh Fruit, 1 or Fruit Juice, ½ c.	1	2	2	2
L Hot or Cold Vegetable Soup (page 16), 1½ c.	½	1	1	1½
Whole-Grain Bread, 1 slice	1	2	2	2
Margarine, 1 tsp.	1	1	1	1
Skim Milk, 8 oz.	1	1	1	1
D Rice Meatballs With Sauce (page 95), 2	1	1	1½	1½
Pasta, ½ c.	1	2	2½	2½
Fancy Steamed Vegetables (page 55), ½ c.	1	1	2	2
A/S Raspberry Delight (page 120), ½ c.	1	1	1	1

TOTAL DAILY CALORIES
(Number of Servings)

RECIPE SERVING SIZE		1200	1500	1800	2100
B	Oats & Fruit Breakfast (page 102), 1 c.	1	1	1	1
L	Salad That's A Meal (page 30), 4 c.	1	1	1½	1½
	Orange-Yogurt Dressing (page 44), ¼ c.	1	1½	2	2
	Healthy Bread Your Family Will Love (page 107), 1 slice	2	3	3	3
	Margarine, 1 tsp.	1	1	2	2
D	Oriental Chicken (page 80), ¾ c.	1	1½	1½	2
	Basic Rice (page 67), ⅓ c.	2	3	4	4
A/S	Skim Milk, 8 oz.	½	½	1	1
	Dry Cereal, 1 c.	½	½	1	1

WEEK 4 DAY 1 MEATLESS Meals

TOTAL DAILY CALORIES
(Number of Servings)

RECIPE SERVING SIZE	1200	1500	1800	2100
B Pancakes With Blueberries (page 104), 2 pancakes	1	1½	1½	2
Fresh Fruit, 1 or Fruit Juice, ½ c.	1	1	2	2
Skim Milk or Nonfat Plain Yogurt, 8 oz.	1	1	1	1
L Overnight Rice and Bean Salad (page 37), 1¼ c.	1	1½	1½	2
Crusty Continental Bread (page 108), 1 slice	2	2	2	2
Margarine, 1 tsp.	1	2	2	2
D Meatless Spaghetti Sauce (page 21), 1 c.	1	1½	2	2
Pasta, ½ c.	2	2	2½	3
Cold Bean Salad (page 36), ½ c.	1	1	1½	2
A/S Popcorn, 3 c.	½	½	1	1
Fresh Fruit, 1	1	1	1	1

WEEK 4 DAY 2

TOTAL DAILY CALORIES
(Number of Servings)

RECIPE SERVING SIZE	1200	1500	1800	2100
B Banana Bread (page 100), 1 slice	2	2	2	3
Skim Milk or Nonfat Plain Yogurt, 8 oz.	1	1	1	1
L Meatless Spaghetti Sauce (page 21), 1 c.	1	1½	2	2
Pasta, ½ c.	2	2½	3	4
Vegetable Sticks, ½ c.	1	1	2	2
D Orange Chicken (page 82), 1 c.	1	2	2	2
Basic Rice (page 67), ⅓ c.	2	2	3	3
Cold Bean Salad (page 36), ½ c.	1	1	1½	2
A/S Skim Milk, 8 oz.	½	½	½	½
Dry Cereal, 1 c.	1	1	1	1

WEEK 4 DAY 3 — MEATLESS Meals

RECIPE SERVING SIZE		1200	1500	1800	2100
B	Pancakes (page 104), 2 pancakes	2	2½	3	3½
	Skim Milk or Nonfat Plain Yogurt, 8 oz.	1	1	1	1
	Fresh Fruit, 1 or				
	Fruit Juice, ½ c.	1	2	2	2
L	Basic Rice (page 67), ⅓ c.	2	3	3½	3½
	Sunflower Seeds, 1 tb.	1	1	2	2
	Skim Milk, 8 oz.	1	1	1	1
	Cold Bean Salad (page 36), ½ c.	½	1	1	1
D	Meatless Shepherd's Pie (page 61),				
	⅛ recipe	1	1	1½	2
	Delightful Fruit Salad (page 39), 1 c.	½	½	1	1
A/S	Popcorn, 3 c.	1	1	2	2

TOTAL DAILY CALORIES (Number of Servings)

WEEK 4 DAY 4

RECIPE SERVING SIZE		1200	1500	1800	2100
B	Oat Bran Muffin (page 101), 1	1	2	2	2
	Skim Milk or Nonfat Plain Yogurt, 8 oz.	1	1	1	1
	Fresh Fruit, 1 or				
	Fruit Juice, ½ c.	1	1	2	3
L	Tuna or Shrimp Spread (page 110),				
	½ c.	1	1	1½	2
	Healthy Bread Your Family Will Love				
	(page 107), 1 slice	2	2	3	4
	Skim Milk, 8 oz.	1	1	1	1
D	Cabbage Stew With Beef (page 17),				
	2 c.	1	1	1¼	1½
	Delightful Fruit Salad (page 39),				
	1 c.	1	1½	1½	1½
	Oat Bran Muffin (page 101), 1	1	1	1	1
A/S	Pineapple Dessert (page 121), ⅔ c.	1	1	1	1

TOTAL DAILY CALORIES (Number of Servings)

WEEK 4 DAY 5

RECIPE SERVING SIZE		1200	1500	1800	2100
B	Sweet Potato With Cheese (page 53), ½ potato	1	1½	1½	2
	Fresh Fruit, 1 or				
	Fruit Juice, ½ c.	2	2	3	3
	Skim Milk or Nonfat Plain Yogurt, 8 oz.	1	1	1	1
L	Cabbage Stew With Beef (page 17), 2 c.	½	1	1½	1½
	Bread Sticks, 2	2	2½	2½	3
	Margarine, 1 tsp.	1	1	2	2
	Skim Milk or Nonfat Plain Yogurt, 8 oz.	1	1	1	1
D	Oven-Baked Fish (page 88), 5 oz.	1	1	1½	2
	Basic Rice (page 67), ⅓ c.	2	3	3½	4
	Marinated Vegetables (page 56), ¾ c.	1	1	1	2
A/S	Fresh Fruit, 1	2	2	2	2

WEEK 4 DAY 6 MEATLESS Meals

RECIPE SERVING SIZE		1200	1500	1800	2100
B	Basic Rice (page 67), ⅓ c.	2	2½	3	3½
	Sunflower Seeds, 1 tb.	1	1	1	1
	Fresh Fruit, 1 or				
	Fruit Juice, ½ c.	1	1	2	2
	Skim Milk or Nonfat Plain Yogurt, 8 oz.	1	1	1	1
L	Pizza (page 109), 1 slice	2	2	3	4
	Tossed Salad, 2 c.	1	1	2	2
	Vinaigrette Light (page 42), 1 tb.	1	1	1	2
D	Lentil-Rice Soup (page 12), 1¾ c.	1	1½	2	2½
	Crusty Continental Bread (page 108), 1 slice	2	2½	3	3
	Margarine, 1 tsp.	1	1	1	1
A/S	Raspberry Delight (page 120), ½ c.	1	1	1	1

RECIPE SERVING SIZE	TOTAL DAILY CALORIES (Number of Servings)			
	1200	**1500**	**1800**	**2100**
B Pizza (page 109), 1 slice	2	2	2	2
Skim Milk, 8 oz.	1	1	1	1
Fresh Fruit, 1 or				
Fruit Juice, ½ c.	1	1	2	2
L Lentil-Rice Soup (page 12), 1¾ c.	1	1½	2	2½
Bread Sticks, 2	1	2	3	3
Margarine, 1 tsp.	1	1	2	2
D Surprise Quiche (page 63), 1 slice	2	2½	3	4
Delightful Fruit Salad (page 39), 1 c.	1	1	1	1
Whole-Grain Roll, 1	1	2	2	3
A/S Banana-Strawberry Milkshake (page 116), 1	½	½	½	½

INDEX

A

abbreviations, inside front cover
appetizers, 65, 72, 85, 91, 94-96
apple, 122-123
asparagus, 8, 55

B

banana, 40, 100, 116, 118
barbeque sauce, 26
barley, 14-15
beans, 14-15, 18-19, 31, 33, 36-37, 68-71,
    preparation of, 59
beef, 7, 17-18, 20
    see also, Poultry, Fish and Meat, 73
beverages, see Desserts and
    Beverages, 113
blueberry, 101, 104, 116, 124
bread, 100, 105-108
bread crumbs, 99
brown rice, 67
burritos, 70

C

cabbage, 10, 17
cake, 126
calcium, 3
carbohydrates, 3
carrots, 54, 56
cereal, 102-103
cheese, 33, 51, 53, 60, 64-65 , 109
chicken, 7, 15, 18, 34, 45, 111
    see also, Poultry, Fish and Meat, 73
chili, 18-19
cholesterol, 3
coffee cake, 126
cook time, 3
cookies, 124-125
cornmeal, 69
crockpot option, 10, 12, 14-19
croutons, 99

D

desserts, See Desserts and
    Beverages, 113
dietary fiber, 3
Dietary Guidelines for Americans,
    inside back cover

E

eggs, 31, 72, 112
equivalents, measuring, inside
    front cover
exchanges, 3

F

fat, 3
fish, 45, 88-91
    see also, Poultry, Fish and Meat, 73
Four-Week Menu Plan, 127
french toast, 105
fruit, 39, 46, 116-125

G

gelatin, 40-41
glaze, 24
Grains and Fillings, 97

I

iron, 3

L

lasagna, 64, 93
legumes, preparation of, 59
lentils, 12-13
lemon, 44, 50

M

marinade, 45
mayonnaise blend, 29
meat, see Poultry, Fish and Meat, 73
Meatless Meals, 57
    see also Four-Week Menu Plan,
    129-135, 137, 139, 141-144
menu planning, 128
menu plans, 129-144
milkshakes, 116-119
muffins, 101

N

nonstick spray coating, inside front cover
Nutritional Information, 3

O

oats, 101-102
orange, 24-25, 38, 50, 82-83, 117

P

pancakes, 104
parsley, 24, 53, 76
pasta, 32-35, 64-66
pineapple, 25, 118, 121
pita pockets, 71
pizza, 23, 109
pear, 41
potato, 9-11, 30-31, 50-52, 61-62, 87, 92
poultry, See Poultry, Fish and Meat, 73
prep time, 3
protein, 3
protein complementation, 4

Q

quiche, 63

R

raspberry, 117, 120
rice, 11-12, 37-38, 67-68, 95

S

Salads and Dressings, 27
salmon, 35, 89, 91
sauces, see Soups and Sauces, 5
scallops, 90
serving size, 3
shrimp, 35, 38, 90, 110
snacks, 72, 85, 91, 94-96, 99, 109,
    116-121
sodium, 3
Soups and Sauces, 5
sour cream substitute, 26
soy, 25, 41
spaghetti sauce, 20-21
spinach, 30, 63, 96
stew, 17
stir-fry, 81, 83, 90
stock, 7
strawberry, 40, 118-119
squash, 56
sweet potatoes, 53-54

T

tofu, 21, 59, 63-65, 72
tomato, 21-22, 60, 71
tuna, 34, 91, 110
turkey, 13
    see also Poultry, Fish and Meat, 73

V

veal, 84
vegetables, 7, 16, 32, 45, 66, 81
    see also, Vegetables, 47
vinaigrette, 41-42

W

whole grain, see Grains and Fillings, 97

Y

yogurt, 43-44

Z

zucchini, 56

MENU *For Life* **ORDER FORM**

Mail to:

HEALTH FOCUS, INC.
P.O. Box 8113
Rochester, Michigan 48308
(313) 375-2130

Allow 2-3 weeks for delivery

Please make check or money order payable to HEALTH FOCUS, INC. VISA/MasterCard accepted. Michigan residents: add 4% sales tax.

SEE OTHER SIDE

Please send me

_____ copy (s) of **MENU FOR LIFE**

_____ @ $14.95 each

_____ + $2.00 shipping and handling (for first book)

_____ + $ .50 shipping and handling (each additional book to the same address)

_____ **Michigan residents:** Add 4% sales tax

_____ Total

MENU *For Life* **ORDER FORM**

Mail to:

HEALTH FOCUS, INC.
P.O. Box 8113
Rochester, Michigan 48308
(313) 375-2130

Allow 2-3 weeks for delivery

Please make check or money order payable to HEALTH FOCUS, INC. VISA/MasterCard accepted. Michigan residents: add 4% sales tax.

SEE OTHER SIDE

Please send me

_____ copy (s) of **MENU FOR LIFE**

_____ @ $14.95 each

_____ + $2.00 shipping and handling (for first book)

_____ + $ .50 shipping and handling (each additional book to the same address)

_____ **Michigan residents:** Add 4% sales tax

_____ Total

NAME _____

ADDRESS _____

CITY _____ STATE _____ ZIP _____

DAYTIME PHONE (___) _____

DELIVER TO: (if different address)

NAME _____

ADDRESS _____

CITY _____ STATE _____ ZIP _____

MY PAYMENT IS BY:

☐ Check   ☐ Money Order   ☐ VISA   ☐ MasterCard

Credit Card Number (all digits)   Expiration Date: _____

Signature _____
(required if using credit card)

- -

NAME _____

ADDRESS _____

CITY _____ STATE _____ ZIP _____

DAYTIME PHONE (___) _____

DELIVER TO: (if different address)

NAME _____

ADDRESS _____

CITY _____ STATE _____ ZIP _____

MY PAYMENT IS BY:

☐ Check   ☐ Money Order   ☐ VISA   ☐ MasterCard

Credit Card Number (all digits)   Expiration Date: _____

Signature _____
(required if using credit card)